IN HIS TIME

JINNI NASTIUK

WESTBOW
PRESS®
A DIVISION OF THOMAS NELSON
& ZONDERVAN

In His Time

A collection of Miracles,
Signs and Wonders that His
believers have experienced
during and since the revival
era in the 1960's and '70's.

Author - Publisher

The principal author, Virginia 'Jinni' Nastiuk, has published several technical
manuals and ancillaries based upon her life's work as a Master Pattern-maker
– mainly for women's apparel.

PERSONAL PATTERNS -- by Jinni
A Manual for Perfect Patternmaking –
ISBN #0-942003-01-2

A Manual for Flat Pattern Design –
ISBN #0-942003-06-3

KNITTING To Your Personal Pattern –
ISBN #-942003-36-5

IN HIS TIME –
978-1-9736-5025-6

Printed in the United States of America

Scriptures taken from the Holy Bible, New International Version®, NIV®.
Copyright © 1973, 1978, 1984, 2011 by Biblica, Inc.™ Used by permission
of Zondervan. All rights reserved worldwide. www.zondervan.com The
"NIV" and "New International Version" are trademarks registered in
the United States Patent and Trademark Office by Biblica, Inc.™

WestBow Press books may be ordered through booksellers or by contacting:

WestBow Press
A Division of Thomas Nelson & Zondervan
1663 Liberty Drive
Bloomington, IN 47403
www.westbowpress.com
1 (866) 928-1240

Because of the dynamic nature of the Internet, any web addresses or
links contained in this book may have changed since publication and
may no longer be valid. The views expressed in this work are solely those
of the author and do not necessarily reflect the views of the publisher,
and the publisher hereby disclaims any responsibility for them.

Any people depicted in stock imagery provided by Getty Images are
models, and such images are being used for illustrative purposes only.
Certain stock imagery © Getty Images.

ISBN: 978-1-9736-5025-6 (sc)
ISBN: 978-1-9736-5024-9 (e)

Print information available on the last page.

WestBow Press rev. date: 5/23/2019

From Ann Margaret Corey

"Hi Jinni,

I have read the entire manuscript and found it uplifting and encouraging. Surely most Christians have had similar experiences with the Lord, but have possibly not recognized those as being actually from the Holy Spirit...showing how big our God is that He can be involved even in little things in our lives. To people like you and I, it is our lives, our additional daily bread from which we gain the confidence to reach out, go further, and be in a state of almost always listening. I remember a Christian friend once who spoke of when God said to Moses to "......go to the mountaintop and just 'be there'."

God is always looking for someone who is listening for His voice. I believe that is why so many of us remain, or have for a very long time, been in a solitary place. We have been in training to speak only when He speaks and move only when He wants us to move. This will get easier as we enter Tabernacles and we will be "known as He is known" for all shall see Him as He is.

Like you, I have had a myriad of experiences in the Lord, especially over the last 49 of 50 years since receiving the Baptism of the Holy Spirit with evidence of speaking in other tongues. Each experience has been indelibly etched in my memory for I have been forever touched by His grace.

There was a time a few years ago when I had grown tired of going to the Bible for answers. The Lord began to speak to me through license plates. I kept a journal of those answers and even told a small group of Christian friends. Soon, though, they got tired of hearing it and began to disbelieve. I realized this was something just for the Lord and me to rejoice in. I guess my sharing so boldly might have come across as boasting.

As of now, I will not be writing material from my life with the Lord for this book.

So, Jinni, I am happy for you that you have taken on this project and believe it will be successful. I have always loved and enjoyed your true stories of how God has intervened in your life.

Love,

Ann Corey"

~~~~~~~~~~~~~~~~~~~~~~~~~

~ ~ IMPORTANT NOTICE ~ ~
All stories are true. The experiences enjoyed
by the authors and contributing writers truly
happened. Some happened long ago, during
God's revival, as early as 1968, while some
have happened as recent as 2017 while this
manuscript was being prepared for publication.

While all the stories are true, we must remind you
that the names and places of most of the experiences
have been changed to legally protect the families
of those involved—even though those involved
have been deceased for many (20 to 40) years.

~~~~~~~~~~~~~~~~~~~~~~~

In His Time

"He makes all things beautiful in His Time. He has also set eternity in the human heart; yet no one can fathom what God has done from beginning to end."
Ecclesiastes 3:11

TABLE OF CONTENTS

Testimonies on which to ponder:
Miracles --Signs-- Wonders

PREFACE

GOD and ME

Oh, My – the wonder of it, all! ! !

My intentions were to start this collection of
God-given experiences back in time
to the fall/winter of 1967/68—
when I first heard about the
Holy Spirit's revival.

But there's another time in my memory that must
be recognized – one from my early teens –
in the summertime when I was laying on my
back on a beach and gazing up into the sky.
There all alone, while watching the cloud formations
change, I was pondering about God, and if He truly
existed like my Sunday school classes had claimed.

Somehow remembering that brief experience,
now at the age of 95,
seems significant as though this was truly
the beginning of my awareness of,
and awe and acceptance of Him.

Through the passing of time I kept a record of blessed
happenings in a notebook, and, though I would enjoy reading
them on occasion, I wondered what I should do with them.

Recently, God spoke this to me:

"It is now, Jinni."

After the passing of so many years, these God-
given experiences are to be shared 'now'.
May they bring encouragement to all who read them.

"Isn't it a small world?" we say when we meet a next-
door neighbor while we're traveling. Coincidence?
I think not! Everyone will have experiences
they may call 'coincidences' but, it's
all within God's plan, and

- - In His Time - -

~~~~~~~~~~~~~~~~~

*Hebrews 11:6 -- And without faith it is impossible to please
God, because anyone who comes to Him must believe
that He exists and that He rewards those who earnestly
seek Him. (NIV)*

~~~~~~~~~~~~~~~~~

~ ~

In His Time

~ ~

MEET THE AUTHORS

Virginia 'Jinni' Nastiuk
Bill and Lorraine Dolan

And the CONTRIBUTORS

"Miss Dixie" Prasad
And there are others whose names have been
changed or eliminated in order to protect their
identity from ridicule or challenge.

~ ~

We have selected a variety of scripture verses that have
been significant in our prayer times and experiences.
Although all of us writers own and enjoy any number
of different versions of God's word, our choice here
was based upon one of the most used versions.

Scripture taken from the HOLY BIBLE,
NEW INTERNATIONAL VERSION® NIV®
Copyright© 2011 by Biblica, Inc.®

~ INTRODUCTION ~

*W*hat you are about to read happened mostly in the Seattle area—during the revival in the early 1960's. Although the strong touch of the Holy Spirit diminished around 1978, the gifts of the Spirit—Miracles, Signs, Wonders—never have altogether quit.

In His Time

"He makes all things beautiful in His Time. He has also set eternity in the human heart; yet no one can fathom what God has done from beginning to end." (NIV)
Ecclesiastes 3:11

*T*he following events happened to people who are now in their nineties, and they continue to manifest in their lives, even today. While reverently recalling the unusual and unique blessings of the Holy Spirit in their lives, they share their testimonies here.

In the following pages, you will meet these co-authors—Bill Dolan and his wife Lorraine, Virginia 'Jinni' Nastiuk, and "Miss Dixie". All testimonies were intentionally held from publication until this time—*In His Time*—they are intended to encourage all readers in their search for Him, and to strengthen God's believers in their faith.

Do not try to imitate any of these experiences for yourself. Each experience is individual and unique; building upon their ministry and maturing. God touches each of His children with His own and unique way of getting their attention—*His special manner of* revealing Himself to them all.

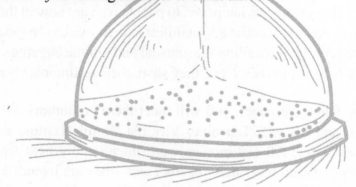

PART

1

Testimonies by Jinni

From time-to-time, for the past 20 years I have
wondered what I should do with the notes I had
kept all these many years regarding God's
Presence, Mercy and Grace in my life.
They include the
Holy Spirit's Revival in Seattle in
the 1960's and 70's.

Then 4 years ago prophecy was said over me that
I should write my story. That word did not
stir my interest until 2015
when a prompting from God came in the
form of hearing His distinct way of speaking to me,

"It is now, Jinni."

~ PRIOR TO REVIVAL ~

God had spoken to me prior to those
early years, too. Date: About 1950
Like when He gave me the name
JINNI to be used in business.
I had randomly opened my Bible, and there it was. Yes.
The name *JINNI* was even high-lighted.

Of course, I have not seen it since then, and neither will you.
But it *was* there...

~~~~~~~~~~~~~~

*Ecclesiastes 4:18 -- "- - that it is appropriate for a person to
eat, to drink and the find satisfaction in their toilsome
labor under the sun during the few days of life God has
given them—for this is their lot. (NIV)*

~~~~~~~~~~~~~~

~ *IN HIS TIME* ~

Although I know I was often a mischievous young girl,
God was patient with me.
God has His way of watching over all
of us, especially those with
a spirit of adventure, like mine.

*H*ere is a poignant example of one incident of my youth. My dad put a tent up in our back yard one summer evening, so my friend and I could camp out all night, we settled in with cookies and hot chocolate.

My best friend, Norma (deceased), also had a spirit of adventure, so we decided to leave our cozy warm tent and venture out to a Beach on Lake Washington for a swim.

My dad thought we were safely tucked in for the night, when we were actually making the one-mile trek and swimming with friends in the middle of the night! My parents never knew. If they had, at the time I may have gone missing, I am sure they would have been most alarmed.

Today's readers may find this adventure an innocent one. But at the time, in the 1930's when I was a teenager, this behavior would have caused parents great concern, and there would have been repercussions. It was not acceptable!

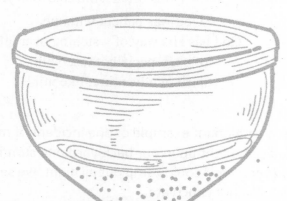

Psalm 139:1-3 -- You have searched me Lord and you know me. You know when I sit and when I rise; you perceive my thoughts from afar. You discern my going out and my lying down; you are familiar with all my ways. (NIV)

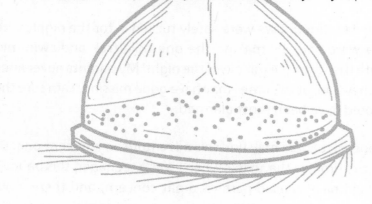

~ *WE WROTE A SONG* ~

The year was 1970

*A*pproximately a year after receiving the Baptism with the Holy Spirit, I heard a short musical phrase run through my mind. That's interesting, I thought, and later that day it repeated, and, for the next few days the same phrase was repeated over and again.

One day when I was home alone that small musical phrase was heard again; so I went to the piano and sat patiently on the bench looking at the keys. In a few minutes I took a pencil and blank music score paper from inside the bench and wondered what would be happening next. I waited patiently.

I did not play the piano. It was in our home because it was a gift from my grandmother for the children to play with.

There it was again! At first, I had to find the correct keys for the tune I had heard so many times before and was hearing again, then mark them on the correct lines. After the notes of that phrase were written down, I was surprised to hear a few words to go along with those notes. So, that day was spent writing the song our Lord God was composing—a phrase at a time with notes followed by words.

After the single lines of notes were written down, next I heard the notes that formed chords. This song was given to me, but not for me alone. It is a message filled with Hope and Promise for all those who believe in Jesus Christ—even for those who are seeking Him...

> Come, My Child and be,
>> and see the wonders of this world unfold before your very eyes.
>
> Now you know My Heart,
>> and start to manifest My Glory set before the worlds began.
>
> It's a simple story true,
> Meant for Sons like you and you,
> For My Love commands the best,
> Though My Child you rest.
>
> The longing of My Heart,
> The Glory of My Throne,
> Creation now is blessed
> For I Am in My Own.
>
> How shall it feel?
> How shall it be?
> When the Sons of God are all come Home.
>
> Peace and Love forever lasting;
> Angels sing a Crowning song.
>
> For this purpose, I have sent you,
> Die but once and die no more.
> Know My Wisdom, Understanding.
> Live and Reign with Me.

~~~~~~~~~~~~~~~

Psalm 40:3 -- He put a new song in my mouth, a hymn of praise to our God. Many will fear the Lord and put their trust in Him. (NIV)

Psalm 45:1 -- My heart is stirred by a noble theme as I recite my verses for my King; my tongue is the pen of a skillful writer. (NIV)

Psalm 47:6 -- Sing praises to our God, sing praises; sing praises to our King, sing praises. (NIV)

Psalm 77:6 -- I remembered my songs in the night. (NIV)

Psalm 119:54 -- Your decrees are the theme of my song wherever I lodge. (NIV)

Ephesians 5:19 -- - - be filled with the Spirit, speaking to one another with psalms, hymns, and songs from the Spirit. Sing and make music from our heart to the Lord. (NIV)

~ *EYE HATH NOT SEEN* ~

1969 – the Baptism with the Holy Spirit.
This experience and especially
speaking in strange tongues came almost immediately
after our first visit to St. Luke's Episcopal Church
in the Ballard district of Seattle.

*J*ust one strange little word *"dimi"* that I had heard in my head started the flow of other words. It was truly amazing to me!—amazing because it simply happened without my doing anything other than to speak that one little word.

In another gathering at the church a message in tongues was given by someone I did not know. I was a first-time visitor to the church—in awe of what was happening. Everyone was very quiet while awaiting the interpretation to follow.

And it came! However, not in a manner I was listening for—from other people. Suddenly 'marbles' began filling *my* mouth, and more were forming in *my* throat; *my cheeks were bulging, and I tightened my teeth and lips as I tried to keep from speaking.*

My mouth was forced open because it could no longer contain all the words. The word of Prophesy poured out saying – *"Eye hath not seen, nor ear heard, neither have entered into the heart of man, the things which God hath prepared for them that love Him." (1Cor. 2:9)*

God had chosen to use me, this somewhat skeptical maid, to speak through. I was the one who needed to be shown, convinced, and encouraged as to the gentleness of His Mighty Power, of His Great Strength, and of His Wondrous Love...

~~~~~~~~~~~~~~

1 Corinthians 1:27-29 -- But God chose the foolish things of the world to shame the wise; God chose the weak things of the world to shame the strong; God chose the lowly things of this world and the despised things—and the things that are not--to nullify the things that are, so that no one may boast before Him. (NIV)

1 Corinthians 2:9 -- However, as it is written: "What no eye has seen, what no ear has heard, and what no human mind has conceived" -- the things God has prepared for those who love Him. (NIV)

~~~~~~~~~~~~~~

~ *GIFTS OF HEALING* ~

In those 1960's Revival days at St. Luke's Church
the Lord's 'Gifts of Healing' were very active.
Father Dennis Bennett was the author of
Nine O'Clock in The Morning.
And, Dennis' wife, Rita, was very active among us.

*T*here were many times that we prayed for and with each other, and healings took place immediately. One vivid memory I have of immediate healings that took place in the basement meeting room of the old original Saint Luke's Episcopal Church is of a woman who asked me to pray for her to be healed. I simply reached out and placed my hand on her shoulder while saying nothing. She joyfully said that she was healed. And later, she asked if I felt anything because she experienced a special feeling that started at my hand contact and ran all through her body; but no, I had felt nothing.

It was not a matter of any of our feelings nor of my faith, but a matter of His Faith that worked through us that night.

~~~~~~~~~~~~~~~

1 Corinthians 12:8-14 – To one there is given through the Spirit a message of wisdom, to another a message of knowledge by means of the same Spirit, to another faith by the same Spirit, to another gifts of healing by that one Spirit, to another miraculous powers, to another prophecy, to another distinguishing between spirits, to another speaking in different kinds of tongues, and to still another the interpretation of tongues. All these are the work of one and the same Spirit, and he distributes them to each one, just as he determines. Just as a body, though one, has many parts, but all its many parts form one body, so it is with Christ. (NIV)

~~~~~~~~~~~~~~

NOTE: After Fr. Bennett retired, he and Rita traveled to 10 nations and missions, and they wrote several more books together. Dennis has passed from this life nearly 30+ years ago but his dear wife continues their ministry through publishing the inspirations that God reveals to her.

Rita's recent book is titled The Lord's Prayer Heals.

Contact Rita Bennett Ministries at:
Christian Renewal Association Inc.,
P.O. Box 576, Edmonds, WA 98020
Telephone: 425-775-2965

Visit Rita on the web: www.EmotionallyFree.org

~ *EASTER MIRACLE* ~

*E*aster preparations at St. Luke's Episcopal
Church included my practicing with the choir.
But, now there was a turn of events where
Bill and I had a choice to make:
1. to stay in town, or 2. drive to be with a gathering of
Christians in Nampa, Idaho. We chose Idaho
because our beloved traveling
evangelist had
asked us to attend.
Little did he or any of us know what God had
in works for all of us there in Idaho.
We were invited to stay in a private home,
along with several more guests.

Day one of the three was something I had never experienced.
Taking place in a Grange hall, were many Pentecostal
preachers and evangelists from around the United States, as
well as approximately 400+ other attendees. And, a nursery
with 20-30 kids of various ages.

Although Bill and I had attended home meetings, and other
one-day events where the hours were directed by the moving
of the Holy Spirit, this 'event' was somewhat more structured.
By structured I mean it started at 10am, recessed for lunch by
12:30pm, reconvened at 2pm. Then, recessed for supper at
6pm. And, at 7:30pm the evening session continued 'til after
mid-night.

Day two I felt like I needed to go home. I was drowning in preaching; and besides, in the morning at breakfast everyone was talking and laughing, and they were totally ignoring me. So, I methodically got dressed, then quietly I joined them in a car for the short drive to the Grange hall—still being ignored.

When we arrived there, it was nearly time to start the praise, worship and preaching for the day. As we walked across the back of the seating area, I saw 'our Sam' sitting alone in the back row of benches. He saw me come in and asked how I was doing. My reply was that I felt overwhelmed, like drowning in all that preaching from the day before. "I want to go home." And I told him of the morning's experience where I was being totally ignored.

Our 'Sam' was a quiet and humble man who was devoted to God with every fiber of his being. He listened so very patiently to the story of my bewildering morning's experience, saying that he had no immediate answer, but suggested that we stay until lunchtime and then leave if I still wanted to. And so we knelt together in prayer that God's Will would direct our way in this matter.

By this time, the hall was becoming quite full, and it was time to begin. So, I walked back to where my husband was seated, and took a chair next to him.

Introductions of those on the program for the day were made—prominent people we had not heard of prior to this event because we were newcomers to this type of Christian gathering. One preacher spoke, then a second preacher from Virginia Beach who was wearing glasses. But these were not ordinary glasses; they were very thick. To be able to read the Bible, he held it within an inch of his nose.

He could not see or recognize anyone in the audience. Even with his glasses on images blended together into a blurred mass.

While he was speaking, he was walking back and forth across the stage with his Bible in hand, recalling the many times he had been prayed for, asking God to heal his eyes. Then he said, "If there is anyone here who knows God can heal - - -." It was astounding to me that *no one* in that vast audience of preachers and evangelists responded!

"Why?" I thought doesn't anyone here *know* that God heals?

With that strong thought still sounding in my head I stood up, put my Bible on the chair beside me, and took one step across in front of my husband.

With that action on my part, God took over! He put into motion activity that could not, nor would not be stopped until He fulfilled it--*In His Time*...

> *The wonderful, beautiful and glorious*
> *Power of God took over my body*
> *and caused me to walk toward the stage.*

This preacher was at the far end when I reached the stage, but he could not see anyone approaching until he returned to where I stood. Meanwhile however, everyone saw what was happening. Everyone was shouting praises to God! Many people standing with arms raised in praise to God! Many people were on their knees! Most everyone was crying for Joy! And, everyone felt the powerful Presence of God. Everyone felt it, and *everyone* was healed! Crippling defects healed!

Eye problems healed! Broken bones healed! *Everything and everyone healed!!!*

He heard the commotion as he walked my direction; he stopped in front of me, then bent down, and I reached up and removed his glasses. Upon doing so, something else most unusual occurred; at that moment of eye contact, it appeared that I was looking through his physical eyes into Eternity... *Glory!*

Nothing was said between us. We had never met. He again stood upright and looked out across the sea of jubilant people and could see perfectly!! He recognized people and called out their names. He saw the children in the nursery and those tending them.

With his glasses in my hand, God turned me around and walked me back to my place beside my husband where He released me. The work was accomplished! God's Perfect Presence was known to everyone!

Commotion continued for quite a while, and 'our Sam' in his humble manner, now *knew* what the morning's bewildering happening was about. *God is here!*—and it became evident that God had orchestrated the activity of the morning at the house, as well as that at the Grange hall!

A myriad of unusual happenings and excitement took place all that day. But this was not the end of the story for me. Not yet!

Later that night, while in bed, a discussion took place in my head—in the spirit world. An 'adversary' told me how wonderful I had been and that my having the 'perfect' Gift of Healing meant I could go into hospitals and nursing homes and heal everyone like I did today. "You can even make beautiful gowns and go on stage like Katherine Kuhlman used to do." It said.

It was a very disturbing night, but finally ended with my telling the adversary what God told me: "This is not a Gift to be played with like a toy. Return it to Me now, and you will be directed to use it again."— *in His appointed time ...*

It was then, and is still my understanding, that other circumstances will occur when and where *He* has planned; and where I may be present. Healings will take place as our Lord God wills them to, and for His purpose; not for the benefit of my ego, but for demonstrating the glorious Beauty, Love and mighty Power of our Lord's presence among us.

Praise to the Lord God Almighty!

~~~~~~~~~~~~~~

Acts 3:12-13 -- When Peter saw that he said to them: "Fellow Israelites, why does this surprise you? Why do you stare at us as if by our own power or godliness we had made this man walk? The God of Abraham, Isaac and Jacob, the God of our Fathers has glorified his servant Jesus... (NIV)

Exodus 15:26 -- "If you listen carefully to the Lord your God and do what is right in His eyes, if you pay attention to His commands and keep all his decrees, I will not bring on you any of the diseases I brought on the Egyptians, for I am the Lord who heals you." (NIV)

~~~~~~~~~~~~~~

~ *GOD-GIVEN WARNING* ~

*T*here are times in our lives when we encounter dishonest people; i.e. con artists and deceivers. This story is about one such incident in my life that, had I not been in close relationship with God, could have ended much differently.

An 'elder' in a neighborhood Christian church, whom I shall call Mr. X, was very competent with computers.

We met when I purchased my first computer from him. A year or so later it needed updating so I contacted him again. He invited me to dinner with him and his wife.

We discussed the progress I was making in self-publishing my first instructional manual for making personal patterns. Then Mr. X proposed that we also computerize my system of Perfect Patternmaking, that I believe was given to me through God's inspiration.

So, we began working together, along with a younger, keenly knowledgeable man whom I will refer to as Mr. Y. Our working together was intermittent and slow, but precise. After weeks, months, even a couple years, the program was nearly complete. But, then I sensed that something was not quite right.

And few days later Mr. X called for a special meeting of the three of us. During that meeting I felt that I was being unduly pressured, so in turn, I pressured God, asking Him to *tell and show* me what was happening.

Immediately, the face of Mr. X changed. He became a total stranger. He was someone I could not recognize. And God spoke, "He's no longer the same man that has worked with you at the beginning." Oh my! How can I deal with this?

The next day I had occasion to go to the office. Strangely no one was there. However, there on the drafting table were parts of our work with another person's name in place of mine. Our work even had a different title. How can this be?

Although I had been forewarned by *hearing* from the Lord, I was now being *shown*. God saw me through it all and showed me their deception. Sadly the relationships and work was immediately stopped.

Our God is always ready, and to protect His innocent, trusting and loving children. His Guidance since that experience has led to the development of the 'perfect' pattern making system that I and our clients enjoy today. MasterPatternmaking.com.

~~~~~~~~~~~~~~

Acts 6:4 - - and will give our attention to prayer and the ministry of the word. (NIV)

Psalm 25:5 - - Guide me in your truth and teach me, for you are God my Savior, and my hope is in you all day long. (NIV)

Psalm 119:98 - - Your commands are always with me and make me wiser than my enemies. (NIV)

~~~~~~~~~~~~~

~ *HOME MEETINGS* ~

Back in those early years of our getting
to learn more about God,
Bill and I would attend many home meetings
where everyone would praise God,
sing, pray and share scripture
and testimonies.

*O*ne particular meeting comes to mind. It was held in a home on the southwestern side of Seattle near Burien. It was a cold winter evening.

As we drove closer to our destination, a light snow began to fall. Because we had traveled more than 60 miles, we were not about to turn around to return home.

We parked on the side of the road just downhill a block from the house. We walked up the gradual incline, picking our way very carefully as more than an inch of snow had already fallen.

At the end of the evening as people began to leave one of our 'sisters' reached in her purse to get her car keys. Not there. She checked her pockets. Not there either. *Oh My!* – no keys in purse or pockets.

I offered to go outside with her to help her look for them. We walked together, arm in arm, on the sloping road down to her car. So much snow had fallen since we arrived and it was still falling—now it was at least six inches deep.

This situation was serious! Where does one begin to look? Perhaps we would find her keys "when the snow melts in the Spring!"

Then a strange thing happened—another of His memorable miracles happened! Without hesitation, I reached down into the undisturbed blanket of snow near the driver's side of the car and picked up a cluster of keys.

Her keys!—and what joy!

~~~~~~~~~~~~~~~

Jeremiah 33:2 and 3 -- This is what the Lord says, He who made the earth, the Lord is His name: "Call to Me, and I will answer you and tell you great and unsearchable things you do not know." (NIV)

~~~~~~~~~~~~~~~

~ PERSONAL FAVOR ~

A friend was so very sick!
It was greatly disturbing for me to
see her suffer so —.
I asked God to "heal her
as a personal favor to me, Lord".

It happened! Right then and there He healed her instantly.
It was wonderful!
But it startled me—even frightened me!

This experience was the first of its kind.

~ ~ ~ ~ ~ ~ ~ ~ ~ ~ ~ ~ ~

James 5:15 and 16 -- And the prayer offered in faith will make the sick person well; the Lord will raise them up. If they have sinned, they will be forgiven. Therefore, confess your sins to each other and pray for each other so that you may be healed. The prayer of a righteous person is powerful and effective. (NIV)

~ ~ ~ ~ ~ ~ ~ ~ ~ ~ ~ ~ ~

~ *WEDDING SHOWER* ~

When I reflect to feeling God's presence among us in those
revival years of 1960's, I remember the joyful
wedding shower we attended for friends,
and I chuckle with God.

*B*ecause my husband Bill and I represented a sewing notions
company we had lots of samples on hand. Therefore, it was
easy to select a gift for anyone who sews.

One item that I selected as a gift for Ruth was a pretty felt-
fabric pocket-shaped cover for a yard stick. It was beautifully
embroidered with flowers. Surely, I thought, she has a yard-
stick among her collection of sewing equipment that will fit
inside this cover. Right?

But, no! Ruth did not have a yard-stick. Unbelievably, that
same day someone gave the bride a *strange* wedding gift—a
wooden yard-stick, Yes!—and it fitted perfectly into the
decorated cover that I gave her.

Who thinks of
yard-sticks and covers as wedding gifts? God did!

It was obvious to all of us that our Lord had arranged this for
our amusement and enjoyment; to remind us once again that
He is among us, even in the smallest measure!

~ *TO BE USED OF GOD* ~

I had a yearning hunger to *know* Him more and *not* to 'play' with past experiences. At times like this I would sing a simple little song.

> *"To be used of God to sing, to speak, to pray.*
> *To be used of God to show someone the Way.*
> *I/We long so much to feel the touch of His consuming fire!*
> *To be used of God is my desire."*

After that, I began an imaginary act *(like a mime)* of eating great handfuls of my Bible's pages, even stuffing them into my mouth much as a starving person might do with food.

Although this hunger faded after a few minutes, it would return spontaneously, almost daily over the next several months.

Over time, I discovered by reading the Bible as well as listening to sermons "— to eat the little book is sweet to the taste but bitter in the stomach —". The meaning for me was that those who go to this 'extreme' will be criticized and berated by people as being fanatics.

Yes, that too has since occurred, but, what choice do we, *or did I have,* or even want to have experienced any differently? You are *(you become)* what you eat. Isn't that right?!

Counting it "All joy - - -."

Psalm 42:1, 2 -- As the deer pants for streams of water, so my soul pants for you, my God. My soul thirsts for God, the living God. When can I go and meet with God? (NIV)

Psalm 84:2 -- My soul yearns, even faints, for the courts of the Lord; my heart and my flesh cry out for the living God. (NIV)

Jeremiah 15:16 -- When your words came I ate them; they were my joy and my heart's delight, for I bear your name, Lord God Almighty. (NIV)

John 15:11 -- I have told you this so that my joy may be in you and that your joy may be complete. (NIV)

Jeremiah 32:17 -- Oh Lord God - - - nothing is too hard for You. (NIV)

~ GOD'S LICENSE PLATE ~

- - RxFife - -

Ann, a single woman about 15 years younger than I, was a very special friend and prayer partner. We had been Christian Sisters in the Lord since 1968. Our profound love and respect for our pastor/evangelist and his ministry was strong. Although 'Sam' is no longer among us here on Earth, we occasionally spoke of him, remembering his encouragement to study God's word.

One day Ann was driving and reminiscing about those precious times together, when a car passed her and quickly moved into her lane. Directly in front of her was now a car's license plate that read "RxFife", like a prescription would read. It didn't take her long to call each of us to share the excitement of the 'coincidental' experience.

A few days later three of us agreed to meet, and to search in a closet where some very old voice tapes of his teachings were stored. As a memorial gesture two of the tapes were randomly selected for playing. We set up the player, poured cold drinks, and set out a bowl of peanuts.

Less than two minutes into the first tape our Sam's voice clearly said "— life is not a bowl of peanuts." Coincidence? We think NOT!! Here we sat enjoying him again, and after more than 20 years, through God, seemed to join in the celebration even with a *bowl of peanuts*. Unbelievable!? Only if you are a non-believer.

Of course, we laughed and replayed that section of tape several more times; amused and overjoyed, and we reminisced over how our lives have been enriched through these Bible studies.

The words of those who ministered to us in the past,
STILL SPEAK.
Amen!

~~~~~~~~~~~~~~

Hebrews 11:1-3 -- Now faith is confidence in what we hope for and assurance about what we do not see. This is what the ancients were commended for. By faith we understand that the universe was formed at God's command, so that what is seen was not made of what was visible. (NIV)

Hebrews 11:4b and 6 -- "And by faith Abel still speaks, even though he is dead."

~~~~~~~~~~~~~

~ *FILL 'ER UP!* ~

A testimony about our Lord's favor toward Ann

60 years ago, at the age of sixteen, I found myself completely alone.

My father had died of a coronary thrombosis when I was eight, and though my mother remarried, my stepfather died of the same condition when I was fifteen. Shortly thereafter, my mother unable to cope, suffered a nervous breakdown. She was institutionalized and undergoing shock treatment at the state hospital across town.

Terror gripped my heart one night as I knelt by my bedside and cried out to God to help me. I wasn't sure if Jesus was real or not.

What occurred after I had prayed was too foreign to my understanding -- I dared not mention it to anyone for fear of the response. My mainline denominational church talked much of faith but little of salvation, but I definitely got "saved" that night. Burdens rolled off my shoulders after that prayer. Colors were brighter, birds' singing delighted my ears, and incredible joy filled my heart! I could not keep a smile off my face, and the happiness of having the presence of the Lord so close was *wonderful!* The secret was to sustain me through the months ahead as I tackled many a task too great for a teenager, never revealing my needs to anyone. At every turn, the Lord showed me what to do.

My mother owned a rental property that was free and clear of debt, so I used the rent money, plus the Social Security checks to make our house payment, pay the utilities, buy groceries, etc. Forging my mother's signature and balancing the checkbook made me nervous. Every penny was important. Only once, however, did the bank statement come with a negative balance, and that was for being only two cents overdrawn! I smiled, realizing my "teacher" was being faithful. The joy of the Lord was always present, sometimes more than others and I found He had a delightful sense of humor.

Though I never doubted divine intervention was occurring in my life, there had been no *human* to validate what was happening to me until one special day I will never forget. Here's the story:

I had obtained my driver's license just before my mother was hospitalized. This was a Godsend, for I went to visit her twice a week, and used her car instead of my bike for most of my needs now. I was a good student, but knew little, if anything, about automobile maintenance. The subject had never entered this already overburdened teenager's mind.

So one afternoon, as I sat waiting for a stoplight to change to green, my eyes wandered to a gas station down the street. It slowly dawned on me that cars need gas. How long had I been driving this car anyway? I honestly could not say. A quick glance at the fuel indicator, which was about a quarter of an inch past empty, sent me flying into the station where I slammed on the brakes at the first pump. I contemplated the gross neglect of my mother's car and how close I had come to running out of gas! Heart racing aside, I tried to appear as "in control" as possible.

A man in grimy overalls emerged from the bays. "Fill 'Er Up!" I said, remembering my stepfather used to say that.

He placed the nozzle of the pump in my gas tank and asked if I wanted him to check under the hood, to which I replied in the affirmative. I nervously gazed through the windshield and under the arc created by the opened hood, to watch his hands first remove the radiator cap. The Holy Spirit's presence began to fill me with peace, but I could feel a giggle coming on as the attendant's head came into view over the radiator. He was getting a closer look inside. Reflecting on the fact my mom had been hospitalized for months and this was the first time I remembered being in a gas station, I had a pretty good idea of what he was going to say.

"You have no water in your radiator!" he yelled.

"Fill 'er up!" I yelled back.

Next the hands removed all the little caps on the battery, and again the head came into view under the hood, as he verified what he was not seeing. This time he walked around the front of the car to where he could see me through the open window. He wasn't smiling.

"There is no water in your battery, either." He announced, stone-faced.

"Fill 'er up!" was my response. The knowledge of how God had been protecting me was increasing. I was having a terrible time stifling a laugh as I observed the increasingly perplexed attendant go about his duties.

Then watching his hands jab the oil stick in over and over with nothing to wipe off, finally drove me into a spasm of mirth. Common sense told him to fill it up. The attendant closed the hood of my car. He walked around to the side to wait for the gas pump to stop pumping, softly mentioned the charges to me, and took my money inside the station. My giggling could be contained no longer, and as he returned my change and leaned his forearms on the open window, I guffawed as he said, "Honey, how did you get down here?!"

I knew of course, but there was no way to explain it. A mumbled thank you was all I could manage. Thank you to the Lord for His faithfulness, and to the man for helping without scolding. The ecstasy of the presence of the Lord was so delightful. I remember leaving the attendant standing in the station, arms limp at his sides with mouth half open in amazement, as I drove away caught up in holy laughter and the joy of the Lord. Confirmation of the miracles happening to me could not have been more evident. Yes, Jesus was REAL, and He had proven Himself to me!

Through the years, there have been many opportunities to trust the Lord, but the basis of my belief in miracles stems from the time He stumped the garage mechanic. He showed a solitary teenage girl she really had a Father who cared.

Sometime later I would stumble across a verse in the Bible that would bring warm tears of joy to my eyes. My precious parents had not abandoned me through any fault of their own, but God had given me the blessed opportunity to experience this scripture firsthand.

~~~~~~~~~~~~~~

Psalm 27:10 -- "Though my mother and my father forsake me, the Lord will take me into his care." (NIV)

~ HIS WORD DELAYED ~

Or was it 'delayed'?

Bill and I did a lot of driving in the sales representative
positions we held. Our driving time gave us
opportunity to pray and talk about
God and the people we
were meeting.
One of our favorites
Became our Bible teacher and mentor.

It was during one of the long drives at night, while traveling
between towns, that I received another word from God.

We were singing and praising the Lord in both English and
our prayer languages when I spoke a message in my prayer
language/tongue. Bill immediately interpreted it, saying
"What is natural to you is supernatural to the world, and what
is supernatural to the world is natural to you."

We wondered, what does that mean? That message gave us
much to ponder and to discuss, but we filed it away along with
many others.

Many months later there was confirmation –

In His Time!

My friend 'Ann' was with me when I flew my Cessna 182 plane to Lethbridge, Alberta, Canada, to join a group of other like-minded students for three days of serious Bible study.

The main teacher/evangelist became delayed and eventually was unable to be with us, so another teacher took over. Within the first few moments of his talking he said, "What is natural to you is supernatural to the world, and what is supernatural to the world is natural to you."

Hearing those exact words now being repeated after so many months was awesome!

Neither Bill nor I had told anyone of our experience, nor of the message. And now to have God repeat His message (word for word) and in another country, through a stranger was truly awe-inspiring.

Of course, I was prompted to share the full experience of our receiving the original message for everyone's encouragement. He speaks today much as He must have done with His Disciples and Apostles; even like He did in the lifetimes of Noah, Moses, Isaiah, John, Peter, Paul and - - - .

~~~~~~~~~~~~~~~

Acts 2:4 -- All of them were filled with the Holy Spirit and began to speak in other tongues as the Spirit enabled them. (NIV)

~~~~~~~~~~~~~~~

~ *DRIVING IN FOG* ~

Driving as much as Bill and I did in our line
of work allowed us time to pray and
praise our Lord, and, to
often experience His response quickly,
in His Unique Way.

One such time happened when we were traveling across central Washington at night heading to Spokane. As we entered a fog bank we began singing a simple praise song and the fog immediately disappeared.

When we stopped singing the fog returned. But it disappeared when we continued singing. Thus, this in-again and out-again experience continued all the way to our destination.

Coincidence? —we think NOT!

~~~~~~~~~~~~~~

*Mark 9:23 – "- - everything is possible to one who believes."
(NIV)*

Jeremiah 32:17 – Oh Lord God - - - nothing is too hard for You. (NIV)

~~~~~~~~~~~~~~

~ NINE O'CLOCK IN THE MORNING ~

Before Bill and I were married in 1968,
each of us was seeking
to know more about God. And, although we
behaved like the rest of the carnal
world, we each had a
deep yearning to "find Him."

After our wedding, we joined a small Episcopal church. We also began listening to Christian radio, even as we drove in our line of work, between towns, states and stores. Among the broadcasts was a 'Brother Ralph' with ministry located in the desert area near Barstow, California, in the very small community of Zyzzx. We decided to spend a "real Christmas" there.

It was at this quaint and rustic camp-like facility that we met 'Fred and Mildred' *(deceased)* from Santa Cruz, CA. They were Evangelist types who enlightened our understanding and knowledge regarding the feasts of Passover and Pentecost.

They also told us about the "unique little church" in Seattle's Ballard district, where Dennis Bennett *(now deceased)* and his dear wife, Rita, had active ministries in the Pentecostal experiences. Dennis Bennett had written a book titled

Nine O'Clock in the Morning

After such a blessed and encouraging time with these God-praising folks, and with 'Brother Ralph' we made fast time returning home to see, hear and learn more about our triune God. We so eagerly wanted to learn about the next step in our walk among 'real' Christians.

I must admit here that we thought we would have it ALL — though it was just a beginning. A joyful and blessed beginning, but a beginning never-the-less. And so it is with fond memories of those early days that I bring Hope, Joy, Encouragement and Understanding to you...

~~~~~~~~~~~~~~

John 3:35 and 36 -- The Father loves the Son and has placed everything in His hands. Whoever rejects the Son will not see life, for God's wrath remains on them. (NIV)

~~~~~~~~~~~~~~

~ *CESSNA N2625Q* ~

In 1968 we bought an airplane in Albany, Oregon.
I became a licensed pilot and continued with the
studies to get my instrument rating in 1969.

*I*n 1972, I flew our Cessna to visit our new friends in Santa Cruz, California. The little airport posed a challenge because of a hill at the north end directly in line with the runway. There was no base operator or other flight and landing assistance except for limited radio usage.

For landing, the customary procedure was to announce over the radio one's intentions of landing to the north, or to the south, depending upon the direction the wind-sock indicated. For take-offs, all pilots simply announced to whomever was listening to the commonly used frequency "Cessna taking off at Santa Cruz"—or from wherever.

That day the procedure became somewhat complicated because another plane was coming around the far side of that hill on the north end, and we were told later that it had no radio.

After announcing my position from the north end of the runway, "Santa Cruz traffic, Cessna on the roll, taking off". I pushed the throttle forward and was on my way. Lift off. Climb.

But what's this?!

Another plane's wheels were within a few feet directly above my windshield. My friends who saw it told me later that they all began "shouting prayers as loud as we could."

My plane had more power than the smaller plane above me. As I leveled off I quickly pulled away from that near-death situation. Which proved to me as I thought about it later, how much God loves us, cares for us and protects us even though we may not always be aware of it. Yes! — every minute of our busy days...

> *Only God! Thankfully He is with us in every situation,*
> *on the ground and in the air. He said He*
> *will never leave us or forsake us.*

~~~~~~~~~~~~~~

Ephesians 2:8 -- For it is by grace you have been saved, through
faith—and this is not by work, so that no one can boast.
(NIV)

~~~~~~~~~~~~~~

~ *UNEXPECTED TROUBLE* ~

During a routine checklist on my plane prior to
leaving for a trip to my husband's home
town, it was discovered that the
alternator needed attention.
The mechanic fixed the problem, and we took off.

*A*fter leaving Boeing Field, we headed toward eastern Washington, Idaho and then to further points east through Montana. It was near the boundary of Washington, east of Spokane, that it was necessary to perform instrument-flying rules (IFR) because of the heavy cloud formations around the mountains. Fortunately, the clouds were not of the storm type.

Seeing that the battery continued charging past the expected period, I became concerned. The mechanic had said there would be charging for a period of time, and so there was. But the 'period of time' didn't quit.

I was now on instruments only, flying my Cessna 182 in dense clouds, and no visible contact with the ground. The terrain below was rugged mountains and wilderness.

As we neared Great Falls, Montana, we broke out of the clouds. Ground in sight, and mountains behind us.

Nearing an intersection on my navigating instruments, I made radio contact with 'Center' to report our position. Immediately after completing this brief report to the Air Traffic Controller it happened. *BANG and BANG! And smoke!* The battery had overcharged. All the instruments that functioned off the electrical system provided by the battery were now dead! Useless!

Thank God that the trouble did not occur while we were in the clouds. I know God had held us safe through that time—even delaying the trouble.

Our journey on this earth was not yet

complete – *In His Time*

~~~~~~~~~~~~~~

Psalm 56:3 -- When I am afraid, I put my trust in You (Lord God, Jesus Christ). (NIV)

Psalm 23:4 -- Even though I walk through the darkest valley, I will fear no evil, for You are with me - -. (NIV)

~~~~~~~~~~~~~

~ MY LOVE EXPERIENCE ~

"Jinni, do you love Me?"
While washing dishes and humming a hymn,
I heard that question. My answer was a
casual "Sure, of course I do."

*T*he question was repeated – "Jinni, do you *love* Me?" But this time I was a little confused by the question, like perhaps Jesus hadn't heard me answer Him the first time. However, I became aware of my answer being more carefully stated, as I stood motionless. And, once again the voice asked "Jinni, do you *truly* love Me?"

It was only then that I fully understood the meaning of the words that He wanted to hear me say; and I wept much as Peter may have done, because I had not given Jesus the response He was looking for. I realized that I had failed the test, although in His unique manner He taught me the various words for, and the true meanings of 'love':

Eros – the 'love' god of sexual desires and perversion. Identified by Cupid...

Phileo – brotherly 'love', as a willingness to help mankind, as shown by gifts to charitable institutions; and even to 'love' all humanity however insincerely...

Agape – God's 'love' for humankind; divine and enduring 'love'. Also, a 'love-feast' eaten by early Christians as a symbol of affection and true brotherhood...

I had been ignorant of their proper meanings and had to learn about each of them by personal experience and not merely through lectures and sermons. He caused me to understand, and to enjoy this experience that I would not have fully comprehended unless I experienced each through the purity of His Power and Mercy.

Our Lord God humbled me! He did it firmly, but ever so Gently and Lovingly, without condemnation; which is His Agape (love) and pure Fellowship that is freely available to _all_ peoples—yes, throughout the entire world...

Praise Him Always!

~~~~~~~~~~~~~

John 3:16 -- For God so loved (Agape) the world, that He gave His one and only Son, that whoever believes in Him shall not perish but have Eternal Life. (NIV)

Matthew 5:43 and 48 -- "You have heard that it was said, 'love' (Agape) your enemies and pray for those who persecute you, that you may be children of your Father in heaven. He causes His sun to rise on the evil and the good, and sends rain on the righteous and the unrighteous. If you love (Phileo) those who love you, what reward will you get? Are not even the tax collectors doing that? And if you greet only your own people, what are you doing more than others? Do not even pagans do that? Be perfect, therefore, as your heavenly Father is Perfect. (NIV)

~~~~~~~~~~~~~

~EVENING WITH MOM AND DAD~

One Friday evening, after supper we were
going to visit my mom and dad for our
weekly tradition of playing Pinochle
on Friday or Saturday nights.
It was just the four of us, and the evening was always
filled with fun, laughter, coffee and cookies.

That night we were running later than usual, and we had to
hurry, so I told Bill to "get the car from the garage and I will
meet you in front" of the house.

I rushed to the bedroom and grabbed my coat from the closet.
I knelt beside the bed and very quickly, while in a rush, I said:

*"Lord, take my hands because I want them to serve you". I
shook them out in front of me much like you would shake
off water.*
*"Lord, take my feet because I want to walk where you want
me to go". While remaining on my knees I shook my feet
behind me.*
*"Lord, take my tongue because I do not want to lie anymore".
I stuck out my tongue, and while making a little sound of
my voice, I shook it.*

Instantly the Lord picked me up and stood me on my feet.

I spoke in a strange language. Yes, out of my mouth poured a foreign language as God caused me to breathe and to speak *supernaturally under His control.*

I *knew* beyond a doubt that God had fully accepted my offerings. *His Overwhelming Love* accompanied this experience. And—I also <u>knew</u> that I was totally and wondrously cleansed.

The experience was Gentle, though
very Strong and Powerful—
and it will forever be encouraging!

Forever, I will Praise Him!

~~~~~~~~~~~~~~~

John 15:1- 4 -- "I am the true vine, and my Father is the gardener. He cuts off every branch in me that bears no fruit, while every branch that does bear fruit He prunes so that it will be even more fruitful. You are already clean because of the word I have spoken to you. Remain in me, as I also remain in you. No branch can bear fruit by itself; it must remain in the vine. Neither can you bear fruit unless you remain in me." (NIV)

~~~~~~~~~~~~~

~ EVEN IN PRISON ~

'Steve' is an only son of a single woman.
When Bill and I
met him he was in jail,
facing severe charges.

His mother *(now deceased)* asked us to pay him a visit. We did, but soon afterward, he was sent to the prison in Walla Walla, Washington, where he remained for several years. Bill and I were permitted to visit any time during daylight and without prior arrangements—"drop in any time".

One of our client's stores was in Walla Walla, making it convenient for visiting at the prison.

Most of the time we drove our car through the territory, but on few occasions, we used our airplane. Also, as the Lord directed, I flew to Walla Walla for the express purpose to encourage him in his Bible studies and understanding. He was indeed, very serious in studies; getting to know and trust in God's Ways, regardless of his current circumstances.

It was on this particular occasion that I flew to Walla Walla with a God-given message and Bible scripture especially for 'Steve'.

After storing my hand-bag in a locker, I was escorted by a guard through heavily barred gates and into an extra-large cell where I waited for him and his guard to arrive.

Although the three of us were together in one cell, the guard allowed us space to talk privately while he sat at a far end with his own reading material.

The unique presence of God was ever so real to us both—that this meeting was *not a coincidence!*

Unbeknownst to either of us, both of us had been studying the *exact same* old testament's prophet and the *exact same pages of this prophet's writings* for several days prior to my arrival.

It was obvious that our ever-living Lord God, Jesus Christ, had planned our day—this very day!—and that He had a special message within this scripture for us to 'take to heart'—like Jesus would say "Verily! Verily I tell you—" because He needed for His disciples to never forget what He was telling them!

Truly awesome !

~~~~~~~~~~~~~~~

Matthew 25:31 -- When the Son of Man (Jesus) comes in His Glory, and all the angels with him, He will sit on His glorious throne. All the nations will be gathered before Him and He will separate the people one from another as a shepherd separates the sheep from the goats. He will put the sheep on His right and the goats on His left. Then the King will say to those on His right, "Come, you who are blessed by my Father; take your inheritance the kingdom prepared for you since the creation of the world. For I was hungry, and you gave me something to drink, I was a stranger and you invited me in, I needed clothes and you clothed me. I was sick, and you looked after me, I was in prison and you came to visit me." (NIV)

Isaiah 55:12 – You will go out in joy and be led forth in peace; the mountains and hills will burst forth into song before you, and all the trees of the field will clap their hands.

~ ~ *"666"* ~ ~

*D*riving with an endeared old family friend across the plains of central Washington, a situation became evident for me to keep alert. This dear old man was forcing himself to stay awake. I watched closely, and whenever his eye lids appeared to begin to droop I would speak loudly to alert him.

Because we were driving in his big, beautiful, new car, he would not allow anyone else at the wheel. My silent, yet fervent prayer to God was immediately answered when 'Randy' *(deceased)* pulled over to the side of the road and said, "Here, you drive!" I could hardly believe what I was hearing!

We traded seats, and although I had no reason to look down at the instruments, I did so, and saw that the trip mileage was '666'. And then a distinct word from God, in that very moment, interpreted those numbers, "Man, as far as he can go without God."

Along with this word came that special feeling of His Presence there with us, Such Comfort! Such Encouragement! Yes, even through a piece of machinery—an odometer.

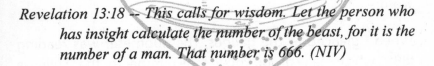

Revelation 13:18 -- This calls for wisdom. Let the person who has insight calculate the number of the beast, for it is the number of a man. That number is 666. (NIV)

Psalm 121:1-4 -- Lift up mine eyes to the mountains--where does my help come from? My help comes from the Lord, the Maker of heaven and earth. He will not let your foot slip--he who watches over you will not slumber; indeed, he who watches over Israel will neither slumber nor sleep. (NIV)

~ ~ "888" ~ ~

*A*nother incident when our Lord God
gave His Encouragement occurred
once again while driving with our dear friend, 'Randy'.

I fervently prayed for our protection before getting into the
car. Our Lord answered immediately! Randy said, "Would you
like to drive today?" Yes! How did he know? I hadn't said a
word.

When I glanced at the gauges, the odometer was reading
'888'; which many of you know is the number for the "Fullness
of Christ's Body".

Our Lord's Comfort and Understanding and Encouragement
and 'Fullness' were right there before my very eyes!

Hallelujah!

~ ~ ~ ~ ~ ~ ~ ~ ~ ~ ~ ~ ~

*Lamentations 3:22, 26 -- Because of the Lord's great Love we
are not consumed, for His compassions never fail. They
are new every morning; great is your faithfulness. I say
to myself "The Lord is my portion; therefore, I will wait
for Him." The Lord is good to those whose hope is in
Him; it is good to wait quietly for the Salvation of the
Lord. (NIV)*

~ ~ ~ ~ ~ ~ ~ ~ ~ ~ ~ ~ ~

~ *WE WILL DREAM DREAMS* ~

All of us dream. We do not always
remember them.
One of my dreams had a great impact.
It occurred one night in 1970.

*B*ill and I were flying our plane to see my son in San Juan, Puerto Rico. We stopped along the way to visit friends, mainly Christian brothers and sisters. One stop-over was scheduled for Bible study at Los Alamos, New Mexico.

The night before arriving there, I had an impressive dream – one which the evangelist/teacher termed 'prophetic', and which he took very seriously as an answer to recent ever-increasing concerns he had regarding his followers and of God's anointed people.

Here is the dream:— I was walking along a well-traveled pathway through a forested area on the side of a mountain. There was a small log cabin ahead in the middle of the path, but there was no way to get around it. I opened the door and entered the cabin, and immediately discovered that I was at the beginning of an underground passageway, and ahead was a wonderful soft glowing light.

As I stood wondering about this, I was aware of my asking permission from my husband to enter a large room to my left. This room was used for preparation of some kind before traveling further through the passage.

As I entered the room, I saw two heavenly beings in charge. Along the wall to my right, was a tall wide shelf-type cabinet with pigeon holes filled with scrolls of paper. All the activities of my carnal life were written on them. Now it became apparent that the purpose of my time in this special room was to *repent of the sins written there so that the scrolls could be cleansed* and put back in proper order.

Jesus came to Earth to show us the True Way, to Forgive us and to Cleanse us of our sins.

This was the message of the dream: My life, like your life, has a plan and a purpose. I knew then that I was meant to teach after my cleansing, in His Name—rooms that no one had taught in before. It is happening!

I have continued teaching in 'many rooms' and to many people since then. Even in our profession, as His Master Pattern-maker, I have encouraged others to stand in Faith and Trust of the Lord God our Savior, Jesus Christ. And there's more to come...

~~~~~~~~~~~~~~

Joel 2:27--29 – I am the Lord your God, and that there is no other; never again will my people be ashamed. And afterward, I will pour out my Spirit on all people. Your sons and daughters will Prophesy, your old men will dream dreams, your young men will see Visions. Even on my servants, both men and women I will pour out my Spirit in those days. (NIV)

~~~~~~~~~~~~~~

~ *TEACHING IN TEXAS* ~

Teaching in Texas, with God's supernatural
protection. Hallelujah!
As was usual all of
these supernatural experiences
were very Gentle, and yet Commanding!

*O*n that day I had a lot of pattern work to do before the
students arrived at Marion's spacious home. On this day her
husband decided to stay home to work in his office. In a while
I took a break and went to the kitchen to fix something to
eat. 'Marion's husband came into the kitchen and we talked
briefly about how the patterns were progressing. But, I had an
uncomfortable feeling regarding this person, and even more
so when he came unnecessarily close to me, even reaching out
his hand to touch my arm. As he did so, his office telephone
rang, and he went to answer it.

He returned quickly and again stood unnecessarily close to
me, and once again the telephone rang, and he went to answer
it. Upon returning, again he came too close for my comfort
even though I moved away from him, each time maintaining
a respectable distance between us. I was determined that he
should go away and leave me alone as I headed back to my
work.

AHA! And, even then as he took a step in my direction, another
wonderful thing happened; the doorbell sounded and several
children selling cookies stood there. Bless them!

I got back to my work at the drafting table, and the husband went back to his office while muttering something about 'getting the message' as he walked.

Oh my! How boundless are the works and protection of Our Savior Jesus Christ. They are far reaching, well beyond our feeble human understanding!

Two days later our Lord God not only provided His Protection, but He moved me into a Christian student's home for three days. While I was there, we talked about our love for God, and of the supernatural experiences we so often enjoyed in His Wondrous Presence that encouraged us to live-in, trust-in, and appreciate His Boundless Blessings.

This experience with the student came about because a thief broke into Marion's house by breaking a huge window which was in a room next to mine. What a mess! Repairs and cleanup were needed. One of the students offered me a place to stay while repairs were going on. I was overjoyed realizing how our Father works situations out, not only for our good, but also for His Glory.

Was all this activity according to His Plan? –Yes! Or was it just a coincidence? –No!

Isn't it truly amazing how all the pieces fit together so well!?—because He did it, didn't He!?

Encouragement – Protection--Perfect timing

~~ *In His Time* ~~

Romans 8:28--30 – And we know that in all things God works for the good of those who love him, who have been called according to His purpose. For those God foreknew He also predestined to be conformed to the image of His Son that He might be the firstborn among many brothers and sisters. And those He predestined, He also called; those He called, He also justified; those He justified, He also glorified. (NIV)

~ *MY DAUGHTER'S DEATH* ~

My precious daughter, Linda Kaye
DeHaven, died July 3, 1994.
It was at her funeral that God made His
Loving Presence known to me again.

*M*any people were already in the Church prior to my arrival. I had waited for a time when most people were seated before I went to see her and to say goodbye. Truly, I wanted to go with her.

The room with her casket was at the end of a long hallway. As I stepped into the hall from the main chapel, I was praying to keep my mind free to receive only a True word from our Lord. I prayed that way because she had married a man from a different belief and she had gone through all the rituals; and I was leary of what I might see.

The women of the Church had dressed her and fixed her beautiful hair. She looked very nice. The very instant I saw her, our Lord's Strong yet Gentle voice said to me, "She knows better now."

Those words have given me His Peace and Comfort, as well as His Encouragement for all other times when my thoughts wander back to being close to her during those difficult final hours—especially at times when I questioned God as to whether she was still a Christian since joining her husband's church—and to the baptisms she enjoyed in her teen years.

"She knows better now."

I do not question the meaning of His message. I have full trust that our God is in complete control. Those words told me that my precious daughter is alive with Him, and nothing else matters.

~ ~ ~ ~ ~ ~ ~ ~ ~ ~ ~ ~ ~

Acts 16:31 -- Believe in the Lord Jesus, and you will be saved --you and your household. (NIV)

Psalm 89:31- 33 -- If they violate my decrees and fail to keep my commands, I will punish their sin with a rod, their iniquity with flogging; but I will never take my love from him, nor will I ever betray My faithfulness. (NIV)

~ ~ ~ ~ ~ ~ ~ ~ ~ ~ ~ ~ ~

~ MY FATHER'S PASSING ~

I was not at home when my father suddenly died.
My husband, Bill, and I were visiting an unique black
church in Seattle where we enjoyed an
evening of Worship and Praise
in their main chapel.

*F*rom the Chapel, the congregation went into other rooms for prayers of salvation and healing. It must have been around this very hour that my father was having a stroke.

When we arrived home around 10:30pm, my brother-in-law called and asked us to come right away to my parent's home.

I was deeply saddened; but I was also feeling guilty about not being home when my mother first called and needed me.

Hours later, we finally returned home. Upon entering the house and walking through the kitchen, I grabbed at Bills chest and began crying uncontrollably. He quietly uttered only two words, "Oh Jesus". Instantly the sobbing stopped, and our Lord's Wonderful and Beautiful Peace came flooding over us.

There we stood for a while—in awe of
God's Wondrous Presence.

Slowly I got ready for bed. But when I laid down, again I began to cry in great sobs. And, again Jesus answered my call and I felt His Beautiful Presence. Finally, I slept with His Gentle and Loving Peace comforting me.

~~~~~~~~~~~~~~

Matthew 11:28-30 – "Come to me, all ye who are weary and burdened, and I will give you rest. Take my yoke upon you and learn from me, for I am gentle and humble in heart, and you will find rest for your souls. For my yoke is easy and my burden is light." (NIV)

~~~~~~~~~~~~~~

~ *MERCY SHIPS* ~

- *Patterns - Sewing - Snakes* -

I drove my Chevrolet XL van from Seattle
to the far eastern side of Texas where
the Mercy Ships organization has
International Headquarters in Tyler.

*T*he purpose for my going there was to serve as a volunteer, and to assist in any way that was needed. It turned out that my job would be to catch up with a huge accumulation of papers ready for filing. With my business experience I could do that easily. The office manager and I remain friends through email to this day after more than 20 years.

Throughout the month I was there, I enjoyed several wonderful experiences. All were profound. The following are but a few:

1. Pattern-making with Hye-Sook - -
In preparation for my trip to Tyler, Texas, I packed my van with a lot of stuff. It was an XL model with a lot of room inside, so why not?

Therefore, I took two sewing machines and a case with everything I would need for hand-drafting basic-body patterns; rulers, pencils with erasures and scissors, including a roll of special pattern paper. Of course, we would also be needing muslin fabric and threads just in case there happened to be anyone at the Mercy Ships organization wanting my unique service.

As I reached the campus after six long days of driving, the Lord greeted me. I felt that undeniable Presence of God as I drove through the entrance-way. His Love and His Peace are always gentle and comforting and here He met me and my expectations for the days ahead with His abundant Joy. And every day while I was 'on board' I would experience evidence of our Lord's Awesome Presence and Direction.

My room for the next four weeks was in a lodge occupied by many other volunteers. I was volunteering for four weeks of general office work, among others who were in training to work in countries where medical assistance is nearly nonexistent, yet is sorely needed.

Some volunteers work with food preparation and general duties in the dining hall. Some were nurses-in-training for serving aboard one of three hospital ships that this organization had at the time, or others were in training to staff a hospital within some foreign country.

A few days into my stay I met three young Asian women. One was from South Korea. She and I shared a common interest. She was a student of apparel design from a University in Seoul, South Korea. I was *(and still am)* an instructor and developer of advanced methods of pattern-making for *all* body types regardless of sizes, ages and posture characteristics.

Her experience and education differed greatly from my system, of course; however, she immediately took to it. Her desire and intent for a future career was to be an apparel designer for *all* body shapes—as I was equipped to teach her. And so, during our after-work hours I taught her how to measure and draft the Perfect Patternmaking method and principals for fitting every body type as God had showed me-- that is, aside from the general basics taught in schools everywhere—even of higher education.

During the times that she and I spent together, one of the nurses-in-training—Marion—became very interested in our project. She would be going to a country somewhere in Africa. Her clothing style would be restricted to certain length and body coverage. And, "yes" I would be glad and honored to make a 'perfect' pattern and dress for her specific needs—but, we needed fabric and thread to match.

2. Sewing for Marion's mission - -
Our plan was for her to buy fabric she deemed suitable. But where? Any town large enough to have a fabric store was many miles away. She borrowed a car and drove away.

When Marion returned she told me about her 'luck' when she saw a yard sale sign. She handed me a package with a piece of pink fabric. Not only was it the *perfect* amount of yardage, it was also the *perfect* color-match to the only spool of pink thread that I brought with me.

No Coincidence!
Our Lord is involved in every thread of our lives.

~~~~~~~~~~~~~~

Mark 7:37 -- People were overwhelmed with amazement. "He has done everything well," they said. "He even makes the deaf hear and the mute speak." (NIV)

~~~~~~~~~~~~~~

3. Snakes - -

It was Sunday. The optional luncheon meal was to go either through the buffet line or take a sandwich in a paper sack and sit outside. The latter was my choice. I wanted to sit by the lake with my Bible.

I had seen the lake from a distance; it was a short walk. As I got closer, I saw there were two sections of the lake, divided by a land mass wide enough for a big truck to drive across.

Knee-high grass and bushes were growing along the top of this land bridge except for a well-used pathway in the center. My mind went into overdrive." Oh my, I hope there aren't any snakes out there!", I thought. So, I walked with caution, stomping the ground with every step I took, meaning to scare them away.

Upon reaching the other side safely I saw there was a small clearing ahead with several folding chairs close to a rugged looking wooden Cross. This was my destination. While eating and reading for the hour or so, I had frequent thoughts that snakes could be in this beautiful setting and ruin my day.

At last, I was able to settle down and enjoy the peaceful setting of the location.

I returned to the main lodge by the way I had come. Of course, being human and female, I stomped my feet with every step along the pathway, meaning to scare away any snakes that could be lingering in the knee-high grass.

Conversation with one of the kitchen volunteers was a doctor in training found its way into talking about the old rugged cross area by the lake. He said that he had been jogging on the wider pathway that surrounded the lake at the same time I was there but he had not seen me. Our talk led to the possibility of there being snakes in the area, even though other people in the know said they "have never seen a snake around here."

Okay? Well now! Just one minute, because Mr. Jogger Doctor said he saw two that day. One was dead on the pathway that circled the lake. and the other slithered off the pathway into the grass and bushes not 150' from where I was enjoying my day. Interesting?!

~~~~~~~~~~~~~~

Exodus 33:14 – The Lord replied, "My Presence will go with you and I will give you rest." (NIV)

~~~~~~~~~~~~~~

~ ICE ON RUNWAY ~

The death of beloved family members happens
to all of us. My husband's
father was dying.

Bill's father was in a hospital with many of his family around him. Bill's sister called us with details, and all of them were wanting us there as fast as possible. I knew that my Cessna could make the 1500-mile trip in less than a day—today.

We quickly packed our stuff in the plane and took off!

It was a cold winter day in Seattle. As we headed east toward Fort Frances, Ontario, Canada, we saw the mid-west was heavily covered in snow. The day turned to night as we flew through Montana and on into the Dakotas; there I changed over from visual flying to IFR— instrument flight rules.

On instruments, I had to keep in radio contact with the flight centers along the way as well as with various base operators. Having yet another hour or so to go, I got a call on the radio from an operator in Bemidji, Minnesota, telling me that the airport at Fort Frances had just had a freezing rain, and the runway was a sheet of ice. I was warned, "Do not use your brakes when you land".

Now, isn't that just great!

With the airport in sight, I descended with reduced speed and flaps down—and with the stall-warning alarm sounding very loud as it should! Touchdown. I didn't use brakes because I didn't have to. There was a moderately strong wind blowing *down the very center of the runway* allowing the plane to roll to a gentle stop *without* brakes.

Remembering this "Miracle landing" reminds me that even when I do not always take time to pray, God has me/us Protected under His Wings!

Bill's brother was waiting for us. When we arrived at the hospital it was nearly 8pm. Bill's father surely appeared to know that his son was beside him because he could communicate through hand-gripping movements.

After visiting among the family, we said, "Good night" and planned to return early the next morning, but that did not happen. A call from a nurse at 2:00am told us, "Your father has passed away."

Bill's father had waited for his son. He had wanted so very much to see Bill one more time. And so, he did...

God's perfect timing!
~~ In His Time ~~

~~~~~~~~~~~~~~

Psalm 91:4 -- He will cover you with his feathers, and under His wings you will find refuge; His faithfulness will be your shield and rampart. (NIV)

~~~~~~~~~~~~~~

~ *GOD'S WARNING IS REAL* ~

A testimony about our Lord's favor, written by "Miss Dixie"

*I*t was Easter.

My husband strongly wanted to stop by and visit some friends while we were on the way to dinner at my parents' home. These friends are Hindus like my husband. We have two children—a girl 17 and a son who is almost 15, both Christians like myself.

I was wondering why my husband was so demanding that we make this detour. These friends were special to him, but this seemed different somehow. When we arrived, I didn't see any reason why we had to be there this day of all days, except I saw a young man, maybe 21, that I was briefly introduced to, and then I was ushered off.

There was a lot of whispering by some younger Hindu girls. Our daughter was always popular with everyone. She is kind, thoughtful and outgoing. Maybe 15 minutes passed, and the young man's mother showed up. I was briefly acknowledged and again dismissed. More whispering. I was very uncomfortable but didn't know why.

Finally, we left and continued to my parents' home. We visited, had dinner, then returned home. My husband had nothing at all to say about the day's unusual happenings.

In the middle of the night I awoke and sat bolt upright. The Holy Spirit told me what had happened! Our daughter was being looked over for an arranged marriage.

I was furious that someone I knew would do that to another family, and on the sly. But then I calmed down.

The next day I called a Hindu friend and she verified that this could have very well been the case but was surprised at the way it was handled. I went to my daughter and told her about the *Holy Spirit* and the friend I had called. Trust among us had been broken. We were on guard after that!

Come to find out one of the ladies was trying to help young men in need of permanent visas or green cards; another way to live in the USA—an arranged marriage to a US citizen.

The *Holy Spirit* showed me that God even rescues us from things we don't know are happening around us, by shining His Light on the dark part of a situation. He is Faithful and True, and is a God who Helps, Protects, Guides, and Guards His children.

We are innocent ones in this world of wolves, but our Lord God protected us.

Our God is so Good and Faithful!
With all my heart I thank You! I praise You, Lord God!

~ *CHRISTMAS IN PUERTO RICO* ~

The winter of '70-'71 -- and an opportunity to spend
Christmas with my sailor son stationed
at Roosevelt Roads in
San Juan, P. R.

*G*ary had been there about 4 months after his year of 'brown water' duty in Vietnam. Preparations for our trip to visit him were started in early September, and our plans included visiting with friends along the way.

Our STOL-equipped Cessna 182 was in top shape, having just passed an annual inspection. And, I had completed training and testing for my instrument rating the week prior to leaving. We were ready...

One stop on our schedule was spending 3 days with a Christian Bible study group in Los Alamos, New Mexico, then on to Mobile, Alabama, for the night. A nighttime landing in Mobile was expedited via IFR.

Next morning—WOW!—took off from Mobile airport in a driving rainstorm. Heavy cloud cover was hovering at 500'. Instrument (IFR) conditions lasted for over 1-1/2 hours, finally clearing somewhat as we got closer to the central area of Florida—and sunshine at last.

We landed at Tamiami airport and called the family group so that we could meet our new Christian brothers and sisters living only a few miles away. They had a private runway alongside a canal where we flew to to meet everyone and to spend the night.

One of our new brothers-in-Christ was an airline pilot home for a few days. He gave us a chart of the area that we would be flying through—ocean and Cuba air-space, and *most important*, a small island named South Caicos.

The entire trip was blessed. And supplying our every need was evident throughout our trip. And, His timing!!—getting that chart proved to be an essential item needed for a fuel stop and for catching our breath—AHA—that's a lot of water between Florida and Puerto Rico. Also, when our flight plan was made it included a stop at Grand Turk, but now that landing was not allowed. Oops!

> *Oops? Because Grand Turk was a military base,*
> *and civilian planes are not allowed to land there...*

As a side note, the radar service at Grand Turk that affects all transponder readings for both military and civilian flight directions would be out for repairs "for a few hours." But, it was still out two weeks later on our return.

When we got nearer to San Juan and talked to the flight controller in the tower, *God's timing* was 'perfect' once again. I was given a "cleared to land" even though our altitude was at 7,000 feet. Unheard of, but a welcomed directive.

I was cleared to land, that is *IF* I could come in immediately, because there were "four heavies" headed to the same airport. Otherwise this pilot in her little single-engine plane would have had to circle around and around in a holding pattern well away from the airport until all four of those big birds were on the ground. That would take a lot of time and use a fair amount of gas.

Absolutely!, was my reply! I nosed my Cessna downward, and I got onto the taxi-strip well ahead of those 'heavies'. There was my son, standing in the rain at the base of the control tower-- waiting for the mom he hadn't seen for several years.

Hugs and tears of joy!
We enjoyed a wonderful Christmas together...

~~~~~~~~~~~~~~

Psalm 91:14-16 -- "Because he loves me," says the Lord, "I will rescue him. I will protect him because he acknowledges my name." "He will call on me and I will be with him in trouble, I will deliver him and honor him. With long life I will satisfy him and show him my salvation." (NIV)

Isaiah 41:10 – So do not fear, for I am with thee; do not be dismayed for I am thy God; I will strengthen you and help you; I will uphold you with my righteous right hand. (NIV)

~~~~~~~~~~~~~~

~ *MY SON DIES* ~

Gary Michael DeHaven—born January 19, 1949.

He was a sensitive child and yet determined.
Sensitive to the needs of other little kids in
school—bringing them to our home
after school for cookies and milk—and
for story reading and telling.
Determined to finish school projects that he
started—getting in trouble in school
because he was 'determined' to stick
with a project; telling his
teacher that he was "not finished yet"!

And helpful, too! Winter snows, with his first
car he helped pull cars out of ditches.
He'd "fix it for them."

In the Vietnam war, he was 'brown water navy'—on river
boats. And, in the DaNang harbor on a repair boat.

In the Spring of 2014, it was first discovered that my son had
Cancer. By then, it was in such an advanced stage, that it
required radical treatment. Strange that the cancer had not
been detected during a complete physical exam less than a
year before.

Chemo treatments were started because the location of the
cancer made it inoperable. After the series of treatments
there was encouragement—but only a little.

Again, Gary's condition grew worse and he was treated with both Chemo and Radiation, but to no avail.

The types of food the family enjoyed was the typical American diet. Likewise, there was the abundance of cookies and candies, containing lots of sugar, of course.

Gary loved pancakes with lots of Maple syrup.
Nutritionally beneficial? No!
But, tasty? Yes!

The nutrition studies that I had personally benefitted from (I will enjoy birthday #95 in January 2018) and doing well (except for surgery to my left hip that did not go well) were mostly from books by Dr. Norman Walker. And making fresh veggie juices from my Norwalk juicer.

Sharing this information with the family doctor and my precious son and his dear wife fell on deaf ears, and I was told that if I didn't stop talking about those healthful food's benefits I would no longer be welcomed. So, I watched my courageous son die. He died a painful, agonizing death.

After all he had been through in 26 years of active military service, it seemed like he had not been given much of a fighting chance to live, was my opinion —...

The night he died his dear wife bore the last of Gary's struggles along with her son by her side. The struggle was over. It was done, and she told me, "— it was terrible."

It was then that I was called to come to say good-bye before the mortician took his body for cremation, February 3, 2015.

Upon leaving their house, God gave me an impressive Sign of Encouragement. There was a full moon low in the clear night sky directly ahead of me on the horizon. I happened to glance at the clock on the dash-board, and it read 5:55am. "5" is God's number for His Grace. Here it was 3 times, meaning His full favor of Grace.

The full moon had thin streaks of clouds streaming downward like tears. His tears and His weeping with me were of special Comfort to my heart as I drove the long lonely road home...

*O my son, my son. Would God I had
died for thee. O my son, my son.*

~~~~~~~~~~~~~~

Psalm 126:5 -- Those who sow with tears will reap with songs of joy. (NIV)

Revelation 21:4 -- "He will wipe away every tear from their eyes. There will be no more death nor sorrow or mourning or crying or pain, for the old order of things has passed away." (NIV)

Hallelujah! Thank You Jesus!!

~~~~~~~~~~~~~~

NOTE:- Karl is the son of a close friend, Donna. He had recovered from cancer via natural treatments at a cancer care treatment center in Oklahoma, and also from the terrible effects of chemo and radiation by adding fresh fruits and veggies to his 'diet'—*AND*—by _eliminating_ *all* processed food stuffs containing processed *sugars that cancers love to grow in*. He was healthy once again.

My prayer is for future generations to become wise and learned from the past examples of other's successes—like the success that Karl experienced.

~~~~~~~~~~~~~~

~ SPECIAL LICENSE PLATE ~

We had known for several weeks that the aircraft carrier,
USS Abraham Lincoln,
would be docking for the
first time in Everett, Washington.

*B*ecause I lived through the WW2 years as a daughter of a Marine Corps Officer, I was naturally interested in such things as big ships and airplanes. Especially planes—and because of my flying days as a Cessna-182 owner. I wanted to watch this 'docking', even if I had to drive there all by myself. It was an important event to me.

The day arrived. The alarm clock sounded its shrill tone, but my body surely didn't feel like getting up so early. Then the thoughts began to run around in my head, memories of our family, and being with my father on various military bases. All precious memories. But my body still didn't feel like getting up at that early hour, nor going anywhere for that matter.

My eyes wanted very much to see the special event happening that was so conveniently close by. But here was a battle beginning between my head and a tired body; between heart and soul.

"Come on! Get up! You know that your dad would love to be with you today, too." "No, dad would understand your 'need' is to get more rest." So, it went on and on, until much time had been spent.

Suddenly my head heard a strong voice; "Go _now_ or forget it and shut up!" I got up!

I got dressed and hurried to the car. Driving, and still talking to myself about whether I should be doing this "all by myself"; "you're a silly old woman"; "dad should be here"; "such a wonderful father I had had"; "do you still want to do this?" Much flooding of emotions and mutterings.

Nearing the base, and with less than 2 miles to go, was an intersection with a stop sign. A car was stopped there. As I came to a stop behind it, I was surprised by what I saw.

The car's license plate: "OTTO"

- - - Yes, "OTTO" - - -

Awesome!

That's my father's name!
How can this be? -- "Otto" on a license
plate? If I had not delayed,
would I have missed this blessing?
Was this just another 'coincidence'? --I think not!!

God did it, didn't He!

~ ~ In His Time ~ ~

~~~~~~~~~~~~~~

</div>

~ TOUCHED AGAIN, JUST LAST MONTH ~

*T*he North Cascades mountain pass is finally reopened for the summer traffic, and I am eager to visit with my grandson and his family living in Twisp, Washington. During this trip I planned to also see 'Susan'. She is the daughter of a close friend, and I was excited to see her because she has married and given birth to a baby girl since I saw her last.

Susan had married, and the family is living in the Riverside area. Unfortunately, a year ago the house that her husband was in the process of building burned down when a fire swept through the valley. Beside my wanting to meet her husband, I was eager to see their precious daughter who was to celebrate her 2nd birthday in just a few days.

Driving toward Riverside, I made a call to tell Susan that I was in the area. She was available, and we decided to meet half way which would give us more visiting time. We had lots to talk about—enjoying pictures in photo albums of their wedding, and of their precious little girl.

At last, we had to bring our visiting to an end, but not until we prayed together—thanking our Lord God for this lovely day.

As I was driving about a mile or so—each of us driving in opposite directions—I suddenly remembered something important that I should have shared with her. Oh my, too late for that now. I would have to tell her via email when I got home, but I was disappointed with my forgetfulness.

Now my thoughts were focused on driving and to stopping in the next town's super market. While in the store I wandered casually through the aisles to find the much-needed items; then made a visit to the women's restroom in preparation for the long drive ahead.

And now, to go to one of the check-stands with my shopping cart. I got in line--and found myself standing directly behind Susan. She had remembered an item that she needed and therefore, turned her car around, winding up in the same store —AHA—and with both of us at the same check-stand and at the same time!

Coincidence?
We both think not!
I was able to share with her the important information
that I missed telling her over an hour earlier.

In His (perfect) Time (again)!

~~~~~~~~~~~~~~~

</div>

Proverbs 3:5--8 -- Trust in the Lord with all your heart and lean not on your own understanding; in all your ways submit to Him, and He will make your paths straight. Do not be wise in your own eyes; fear the Lord and shun evil. This will bring health to your body and nourishment to your bones. (NIV)

<div align="center">

~~~~~~~~~~~~~~~

~ *AM I DONE?* ~

Is God done with me?

Meaning of 'done' being finished and/or washed up –
like quit.
My age, as of January 2018, is 95.

Is God done with you? Or is His Grace and working with
building your faiths and understanding of Him
and His Ways just now beginning?

~ ~ ~ ~ ~ ~ ~ ~ ~ ~ ~ ~ ~ ~

*Psalm 92:12-15 – The righteous will flourish like a palm tree,
they will grow like a cedar of Lebanon; planted in the
house of the Lord, they will flourish in the courts of
our God. They will still bear fruit in their old age, they
will stay fresh and green, proclaiming, "The Lord is my
upright; he is my Rock, and there is no wickedness in
Him." (NIV)*

*Acts 14:22 -- - - - strengthening the disciples and encouraging
them to remain true to the faith. "We must go through
many hardships to enter the Kingdom of God," they said.*

~ ~ ~ ~ ~ ~ ~ ~ ~ ~ ~ ~ ~ ~

PART

2

Testimonies by Bill and Lorraine Dolan

The Dolans are living in a senior retirement center
-- BROOKDALE -- in Stanwood, Washington.

*T*he stories that they share with us here are happenings in
their everyday lives that had their beginnings in the 1970s.
Even last week-end, they prayed for me, and the pain I had
in the left side of my neck for three+ months
began fading and was totally gone within
less than five minutes.

Lorraine had experienced the baptism with the Holy Spirit
in 1972. Since then she has prayed for people in various
facilities:— hospitals, churches, retirement homes and private
homes...

She was president of the Women's Aglow Fellowship in the
Burien area during 1975.

Although she experienced a stroke a little more than four
years ago, her recovery is progressing nicely.

Bill has been part of a Catholic Church Healing Ministry located in Seattle since 1973.

The Visiting Angels who assist with caring for Lorraine, and helping to keep their apartment tidy, are receivers of God's healings as related in this section.

~~~~~~~~~~~~~~

~ TESTIMONY OF HEALING ~

In 1978 the Catholic Charismatic Organization
held a conference at the Seattle Center.

On the first day of the conference a long-time friend of my wife greeted us. She told us that she was seated with a woman who had brought her 3-week-old baby for healing. The baby had been affected by the prescription drug Thalidomide and was born without the sinews and tendons connecting the leg muscles to the bones. Both legs were affected.

Because the main speaker was about to come onto the stage. I told Lorraine's friend that we would pray for the baby after the service; but the friend told us that the lady had to leave before the service was over.

If we were going to pray we had to act immediately. I told my wife's friend to hurry and bring the mother and the baby to us. The friend ran back and brought the mother and her baby to us where we were standing close to the stage.

My wife, Lorraine, came to help me pray for the baby. The baby was laying in an infant seat the mother was holding. When I placed my hands on the baby's legs, her little body jerked and lifted 2 or 3 inches. My wife's friend said excitedly "that must be the action of the Holy Spirit."

We found out later that the missing parts were instantly, miraculously provided by the Lord. My amazement over this event caused me to be concerned as whether I had remembered the healing correctly. But five years later we were sitting in my car in a church parking lot where my wife was invited to speak.

While we were waiting for the church to open, a lady drove up and parked near us. She got out of the car and I recognized her as the mother of the baby that we had prayed for five years before. The mother told us that her daughter just had her fifth birthday; and said that her daughter was "the most coordinated and athletic member of the family."

~~~~~~~~~~~~~~

Mark 9:23 -- - - said Jesus. "Everything is possible to one who believes." (NIV)

~~~~~~~~~~~~~~

~ HEALED OF ALCOHOLISM ~

My wife, Lorraine, was president of a chapter of Women's Aglow Fellowship. This gave her opportunities to speak at conferences, churches, and weekend retreats.

In the 1980s, she was invited to speak at a church in Silverdale, Washington. After her talk, we were asked to minister in prayer to women with special needs.

One lady came for prayer for guidance. Her husband had been an alcoholic for fifteen years. During his alcoholic rages, he would be violent towards anyone. His two sons were so afraid of their father that they left home to live with a friend.

The lady wanted God's guidance as to whether she should leave her husband or continue to live with him. She told me that there were times when she thought her life was in danger. I perceived that her husband had a demon of alcoholism. I took authority to cast out the demon and prayed for God's guidance for her.

Sometime later, she phoned us to say that when she arrived home, her husband greeted her and told her he had a "strange experience." He no longer had a desire for alcohol.

He then went to find his two sons and told them that he was very sorry for causing so much trouble. The sons returned home, and the family was restored to loving relationships.

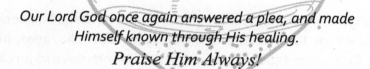

Our Lord God once again answered a plea, and made Himself known through His healing.

Praise Him Always!

James 4:7 and 8 – Submit yourselves, then, to God. Resist the devil, and he will flee from you. Come near to God and He will come near to you. (NIV)

~ *JESUS HEALS IN OUR APARTMENT* ~

*A*bout a year ago—2015—one of our Visiting Angels called to tell me that she would not be coming to work for several days. She said she had a cyst on one of her ovaries, and a surgeon was going to remove it the next day.

I asked her if she wanted Lorraine and I to pray for her recovery. She said she would "certainly appreciate having prayers for the surgery."

When the doctor examined our
Visiting Angel prior to
surgery
he found no sign
of the cyst. The Lord had healed her.

The Lord removed it, didn't He!

~~ *In His Time* ~~

In Praise of Wisdom

Proverbs 8:4-8 – "To you, O people, I call out; I raise my voice to all mankind. You who are simple, gain prudence; you who are foolish, set your hearts on it. Listen, for I have trustworthy things to say; I open my lips to speak what is right. My mouth speaks what is true, for my lips detest wickedness. All of the words of my mouth are just; none of them is crooked or perverse." (NIV)

~ JESUS HEALS AGAIN AT OUR APARTMENT ~

One of our Visiting Angels was a young Philippino girl. She would come into our apartment singing, dancing and hugging my wife.

However, one day she came to us sad and depressed. I said to her, "Laura, why are you so sad?" She replied that her doctor had discovered a three-inch tumor in the left side of her neck; now she was afraid to have the tumor removed. We asked her if she wanted Lorraine and I to pray for her.

She wanted that very much. So, we prayed for her.

During the preparation for the surgery the surgeon discovered there was no longer a tumor in her neck. The Lord removed it with no sign that it had ever existed.

God did it yet again, didn't He?

~~ In His Time ~~

~~~~~~~~~~~~~

Psalm 29:2 -- Ascribe to the Lord the glory due his name; worship the Lord in the splendor of His holiness." (NIV)

~~~~~~~~~~~~~

~ NECK BRACE ~

*A*n elderly couple eats their meals in the restaurant at the apartments where we also frequent and enjoy our meals. They are very friendly and greet us warmly where-ever and whenever they see us.

Recently I noticed he had a cloth collar around his neck. I asked what the purpose of the collar was, and he said that he had a lot of pain in his neck.

The doctor was unable to help him, except to give him the collar to wear. He said he was in constant pain, but the collar prevented his neck from getting too far out of alignment, and he was getting a bit of relief from the intense pain.

I asked him if he would like for my wife and I to pray for him. And, right there in the restaurant, we prayed a brief prayer.

Several days later in Church, after the service we were talking to friends. The elderly couple waited until we were free and said that he had something to tell me. He told me that immediately after praying for him the pain stopped.

He no longer had to wear the collar. His neck was healed.

Thank You, Jesus!

Psalm 96:2-3 – Sing to the Lord, praise His name; proclaim His salvation day after day. Declare His glory among the nations, His marvelous deeds among all peoples. (NIV)

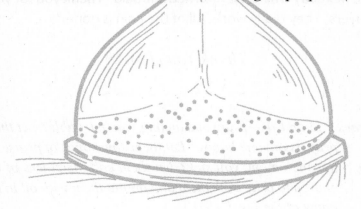

~ ANGELS' CAR ACCIDENT ~

Lorraine and I have Visiting Angels come to our apartment to provide household services for us. One day one of the Angels was coming to work when her car hit black ice on the highway, went out of control and smashed into the car in front of hers. Her car was totaled, and she had severe pain in her back, legs, arms and shoulders.

She was not able to come to work for several days. When she returned to work, she had so much pain that she could not stoop down or bend over to pick things up off the floor.

We asked Roberta if she wanted us to pray for her, and she said Yes. So, we prayed for her before she left our apartment. The next day when she returned she said "Thank you for your prayers. They really work. All of the pain is gone."

Thank You, Jesus!

~ ~ ~ ~ ~ ~ ~ ~ ~ ~ ~ ~ ~ ~

James 5:13 and 14 – Is anyone among you in trouble? Let them pray. Is anyone happy? Let them sing songs of praise. Is anyone among you sick? Let them call the elders of the church to pray over them and anoint them with oil in the name of the Lord. (NIV)

~ ~ ~ ~ ~ ~ ~ ~ ~ ~ ~ ~ ~ ~

~ NEVER TOO LATE ~

Several years ago, our family was staying at the
Warm Beach Park
and we met a man who had an arm that had been
paralyzed for thirty years.

I prayed for his arm and it was immediately
healed—restored to full use...

Thank You, Jesus!

~~~~~~~~~~~~~~

Everything Has Its Time!

*Ecclesiastes 3:1-8 – There is a time for everything, and a season
for every activity under the heavens: a time to be born
and a time to die, a time to plant and a time to uproot, a
time to kill and a time to heal, a time to tear down and a
time to build, a time to weep and a time to laugh, a time
to mourn and a time to dance, a time to scatter stones
and a time to gather them, a time to embrace and a time
to refrain from embracing, a time to search and a time
to give up, a time to keep and a time to throw away, a
time to tear and a time to mend, a time to be silent and
a time to speak, a time to love and a time to hate, a time
for war and a time for peace. (NIV)*

~~~~~~~~~~~~~~

~ RECEIVING THE HOLY SPIRIT ~

*A*t the same camp I met an older man who said that
he was a member of a
Pentecostal Church for 20 years.

He liked his church, but he had one big disappointment in his experience with it. He wanted to be baptized with the Holy Spirit, with speaking in tongues. However, he was never able to receive this spiritual gift that Jesus promised would be sent after His resurrection.

I asked him if he still wanted to receive this gift, and he said yes. So then, I took him through some instructions, prayed for him and he immediately started speaking in tongues.

*The man was overcome with JOY and thanked us
for praying for him.*

Praise Jesus!

Acts 1:17 -- "In the last days, God says, I will pour out my (Holy) Spirit on all people." (NIV)

Acts 4:25 -- "You spoke by the Holy Spirit through the mouth of your servant, our father David- - "(NIV)

Acts 4:31b -- And they were all filled with the Holy Spirit and spoke the word of God boldly. (NIV)

Acts 11:24 – He was a good man, filled with the Holy Spirit and faith, and a great number of people were brought to the Lord. (NIV)

Acts 15:8 -- God who knows the heart, showed that He accepted them, by giving the Holy Spirit to them, just as He did to us. (NIV)

~ THE GLOVES ARE OFF ~

*T*he cleaning lady at our apartments is very busy.
And, she uses both of her hands
on all her work.

One day I asked her why she always wore black gloves. She explained to me that she had arthritis in both of her hands and that these special gloves had threads of copper embedded throughout the fabric that gave her some relief.

Then I asked if she wanted prayer for this condition. She said Yes, so I prayed for her hands that day.

It was some days later that I noticed she was not wearing the gloves. I asked about this, and she said that after I prayed for her the pain left her hands and did not return.

I checked with her several times after that and each time she said the arthritis pain never returned.

Thank you, Jesus!

~ ~ ~ ~ ~ ~ ~ ~ ~ ~ ~ ~ ~

Romans 15:17 -- Therefore I glory in Christ Jesus in my service to God. (NIV)

~ ~ ~ ~ ~ ~ ~ ~ ~ ~ ~ ~ ~

~ MY SON GROWS ~

My son, Darrell, in his early years was short and he seemed not to be growing normally.

One evening while attending a prayer meeting in a Catholic Church a minister, 'Wayne', prayed for a woman that had one short leg. He commanded the leg to grow longer. The leg immediately grew out to match the same length as the other leg.

The same minister was teaching a prayer group in a private home in Burien. Lorraine and I attended this group weekly. Darrell asked if he could go with us to this prayer meeting, so he could be prayed for to grow taller. We said No, because the children of the host did not attend the prayer meeting.

One evening while traveling to the meeting, we stopped for a red traffic light. At this point we were only one-half block from our friend's residence. At the traffic stop, my son popped up from below the back seat. He had wanted so much to go to the meeting and to be prayed for to increase his height.

Since it was about fifteen miles back to our home in West Seattle, we would have missed the meeting if we took him back home. So, we took him to the meeting with us.

We told 'Wayne' that Darrell wanted him to pray for him to increase his height. And Wayne said "Sure, we will pray for him in the group." I said I didn't want to do this in a group, but that we wanted to go to a private area. The host had an unoccupied bedroom that we could use. So, we all went there.

I was very suspect of this ministry, whether it was valid or trickery. But Wayne sat Darrell on a chair. I stood where I was able to see whatever he did. Wayne examined Darrell's legs and he said, "Did you know that one of his legs is about three inches shorter than the other?" I said that I did not know this.

Then I remembered that we bought him a bike--one that needed to be assembled. I put the bike together and asked Darrell to take a ride to see how he liked it.

He returned after the test ride and said that he liked the bike, but it had one short pedal. I said, "Sit straight on the seat and there wouldn't be a problem." Now, I suddenly realized that Darrell surely did have a short leg. He also skipped rather than run when he needed to go someplace quickly.

When Wayne commanded the short leg to grow out, it extended about four inches. Wayne didn't worry about this. As he continued to pray, both legs became the same length, just as he said they would.

Amazingly, with this procedure Darrell gained about one inch in height. And after that I decided to pray that he would grow even taller. At that time, he was not growing naturally at all.

I made a scale of inches and stuck it to the bedroom wall. Every day I commanded his height to increase. Some days it would increase only one quarter inch, other days it would increase an inch. By the end of the year the chart shows that Darrell grew twelve inches.

Thank you, Lord Jesus!

~~~~~~~~~~~~~~~

O *for a thousand tongues to sing*
My great Redeemer's praise!
The Glories of my God and King
The triumphs of His Grace.
Charles Wesley

~~~~~~~~~~~~~~~

~ OUR FIRST FAMILY HEALING ~

*W*hen our daughter, Theresa, was eight years old, she had recurring styes on her right eye. The flesh around the eye would become so red and swollen that she could not see out of her eye.

At about the time one sty was healed, a new sty
would swell in her eye again.

From the time we started praying for the removal of the styes, she had experienced four episodes involving styes. The last time we prayed for her, the styes were healed permanently. Theresa told me this week, that she's not had another sty since.

Praises be to our Lord, Jesus!!

~ ~ ~ ~ ~ ~ ~ ~ ~ ~ ~ ~ ~

*Mark 1:34 — - -and Jesus healed many who had various diseases.
He also drove out many demons - - (NIV)*

~ ~ ~ ~ ~ ~ ~ ~ ~ ~ ~ ~ ~

~ PERSISTENT PRAYER ~

*O*ne Sunday I went early to the prayer group at Blessed Sacrament Church in North Seattle. My co-leader approached me when I came in and said that he and two others were praying for another member.

'Alice' had a lump on the back of her neck about the size of a small egg. He asked for me and my wife to join in with the group in praying for her.

He told us that they had already been praying for several minutes, and it seems like the lump was getting a little smaller. As we all continued to pray, we watched the lump slowly become smaller and smaller until it totally disappeared!!

Praise be to Jesus, our Merciful Lord!

~~~~~~~~~~~~~~

2 Chronicles 16:9 – For the eyes of the Lord range throughout the earth to strengthen those whose hearts are fully committed to Him. (NIV)

~~~~~~~~~~~~

~ PHILIPPINO FAITH ~

*O*ver 30 years ago Lorraine and I were invited to speak at a church in Honolulu, Hawaii. All the members were Philippino— very friendly and full of faith.

After Lorraine spoke, the leader of a woman's prayer group asked us to pray for one woman who had cancer throughout her entire body. This was a big challenge for us, but we and the whole group prayed with all the faith we had.

Several days later we left Honolulu and returned home. About two weeks later we received a call from the prayer group leader telling us that the lady we prayed for was "*completely and totally healed*".

Praise Him!

~~~~~~~~~~~~~~~~

John 12:26 – Whoever serves me (Jesus Christ) must follow me; and where I am, my servant also will be. My Father will honor the one who serves me. (NIV)

~~~~~~~~~~~~~~~~

~ BELIEVE PSALM #91 ~

*W*e owned an auto repair center for ten years in West Seattle, Washington. The business was thriving. We needed truckloads of parts two or three times per week. At times we received so many parts that we filled all the storage cabinets. Stacking boxes of excess parts on the floor was not an option because the state inspectors could fine us for safety violations.

However, there was vacant space in the attic. It was not convenient because it had no stairway to access the space, so we used a ten-foot step ladder to get parts up into that area.

One day I was on the ladder putting four truck air-filters away. Being in a hurry, I failed to completely close the lock on the ladder; the ladder collapsed and shot out from under me.

My body was in a horizontal position 8' above the cement floor, in mid-air. During the fall to the floor I had a strange experience. Everything around me disappeared and I felt a powerful force letting me down very slowly—AND—I felt the strong Presence of the Lord.

My body gently contacted the cement floor; there was neither pain nor damage. Immediately Psalm #91 came to my mind. That scripture states that God would send Angels to deliver us in time of need. And so He did...

Praises be to our Lord Jesus!

Psalm 91:9-12 – If you say, "The Lord is my refuge," and you make the Most High your dwelling, no harm will overtake you, no disaster will come near your tent. For He will command His angels concerning you to guard you in all your ways; they will lift you up in their hands so that you will not strike your foot against a stone. (NIV)

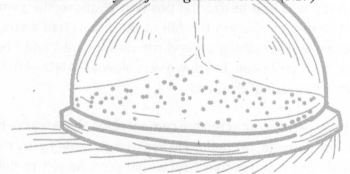

~ BYE, BYE STEEL RODS ~

A few years ago, a longtime friend asked Lorraine and me to minister for a weekend at a Women's retreat. After the retreat, our friend asked if we would stop to pray for a woman while we were on our way home.

We stopped to visit with this lady for a short time. She told us that she had severe back problems that caused her a great deal of pain, telling us how the surgeons had operated on her spine and inserted two steel rods, one on each side of her spine. The rods were attached to her spine by silver wire.

Lorraine and I prayed for her healing, and then we continued our drive home.

A short time later, I received a call from our friend saying that she received a call from the lady with the back problems. She told our friend that after we prayed, she felt an "unusual sensation" in her back.

So then, she went to see her doctor, and he took an X-Ray of her back. The X-Ray showed that the two metal rods and silver wire were *gone!--no longer needed!*

They had been removed and replaced by the Lord!
Thank you, Jesus!

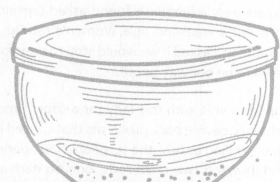

Jesus healed Peter's mother-in-law

Matthew 8:14-15 "- - Jesus came to Peter's house, He saw his wife's mother laid down, and sick of a fever. He touched her hand, and the fever left her, and she got up and began to wait on Him." (NIV)

~ CROSSED-EYES HEALED ~

Several years ago, my son-in-law, Randy,
asked me if I would be willing to
pray for a friend of his.

He told me that when his friend was about six years old,
his mother announced to the family that she was leaving the
family to live with her friend.

The emotional shock of this announcement caused him to be
so emotionally disturbed and traumatized that he became
cross-eyed.

Randy brought his friend to our home in West Seattle. We
prayed for his eyes and they were immediately restored and
brought back into normal position and perfect vision.

How Perfect is our Lord's Love for us!

~~~~~~~~~~~~~~

*John 9:11 "The man they call Jesus made some mud and put it
on my eyes. He told me to go to Siloam and wash. So I
went and washed, and then I could see." (NIV)*

~~~~~~~~~~~~~~

More Crossed-eyes Healed ~ ~ ~

'Steve' remained a close friend with our family. He became a roofer by trade, and had his own business. He looked at the roof on our house and said it needed to be replaced and offered to replace it—supply all the materials and labor—*all for free*.

My wife, Lorraine, felt that this was too much to receive from him since all we did was to pray for his eyes to be healed. And so, we turned down his offer which would have cost him several thousand dollars.

But then we received a letter from him stating that he was very disappointed that we had not taken him up on his offer. Lorraine told me that she was shocked that he was so offended that we did not accept his offer. Since he felt so rejected by our turn-down of his offer, Lorraine told me to contact him and to tell him we will gratefully accept his kind offer. So he came with his crew and replaced our roof. It was a good job that lasted 25 years!!

Shortly after the roof was replaced, Steve invited us to his wedding at Blessed Sacrament Church. We were guests of honor at this fabulous event.

Later in the month I had occasion to give a testimony of his healing at our church. A member of our prayer group asked if I would pray for her son who also had problems with crossed eyes. I said I would be glad to.

The following Sunday she brought her son who was home on leave from the Navy. The entire prayer group gathered around him praying for her beloved son's eyesight. Even as we prayed, his eyes straightened, and became normal and perfect again.

~ ~ ~ ~ ~ ~ ~ ~ ~ ~ ~ ~ ~ ~

And He made the blind man to see, didn't He?
Oh, yes, He did!
All Glory and Praise be to our Lord God,
Jesus Christ!

~ ~ ~ ~ ~ ~ ~ ~ ~ ~ ~ ~ ~ ~

~ *SICK OR DYING PETS* ~

Will God bother to heal our
sick or dying pets?

Several years ago, at our Blessed Sacrament Church's Prayer Group, my co-leader came to me and said: "Bill, there is a young girl here who wants us to pray for her sick dog." She wants us to lay hands on it and bless her dog.

I asked her if her dog was a Doberman Pincer, and she replied that it was. I said that I am very concerned about laying my hands on *any* Doberman Pincer.

I told her how that very week a Doberman Pincer dog came after me when I was on my motorcycle and sank his teeth into the calf of my right leg.

The girl said that her dog was unable to bite me because the dog was so sick that it had not moved in two days.

Relieved by her statement, all three of us went to her van in the church parking lot. She opened the sliding door of the van and I leaned in to pray. The dog showing no signs of life, but I blessed the dog with oil, laid hands on it, and commanded it to be healed.

The next Sunday the girl came to our prayer meeting. She told us that when she got home and opened the van's door, the dog jumped out, ran up the path to the house, and gobbled down the bowl of dried food that had been on the porch for several days. She said the dog was completely healed.

She had one more request for her dog. The Kennel Club that she belonged to was about to have a large event for K9 competition. Her dog was a TRACKER, so she wanted us to pray for her dog to win the event.

After the event, she called to say that her dog took first place in the Tracking competition--and she thanked us for our prayers.

And--We thanked Our Lord, Jesus Christ, for His answers to our prayers.

~~~~~~~~~~~~~~~

More How God Heals Our Pets ~ ~ ~

Jennifer, our Visiting Angel, told me a sad story about a cat she named, Tuffy. She said that while at home one day, she heard a scratching and meowing noise at the front door. When she opened the door, she saw a cat that had apparently been hit by a car. He was all bloody and appeared to have a broken tail. The cat was such a mess that she shut the door.

The cat came to the door a second time—scratching and crying—wanting to get inside. Again, Jennifer shut the door, hoping that the cat would just go away. But he would not, and the third time Jennifer brought the cat in and she washed away all the dirt and blood from his fur. She and that *tough* little cat have now become good friends.

Several years later Tuffy became very sick with a lung problem. She took it to a veterinarian who said that the cat was dying, and he offered to give it a shot to put it out of his misery. Jennifer told him she wasn't ready to give him up.

The next day or two following, when Jennifer came to work in our Warm Beach apartment, she told me the whole story of Tuffy. I asked her if she wanted Lorraine and me to pray for her cat to be healed. She said YES, she would like that. So, we prayed for healing her cat.

Later, the next day when she went home, Tuffy jumped out of his bed, ran over to his food and "he ate the whole dish-full."

Tuffy was healed, and continues to be Jennifer's close friend.

~ ~ ~ ~ ~ ~ ~ ~ ~ ~ ~ ~ ~ ~ ~ ~

Distance Means Nothing to God ~ ~ ~

*O*ne evening at our prayer meeting, our prayer leader told me that he had just received a phone call from his daughter living in New Jersey. She told him that her dog that she so dearly loved was dying, and would we pray for her dog? So, we prayed in our meeting.

The following day Gene received another phone call from his daughter saying that her dog was now healed.

~ ~ ~ ~ ~ ~ ~ ~ ~ ~ ~ ~ ~

Isaiah 33:13 -- You who are far away, hear what I have done; you who are near, acknowledge my power! (NIV)

~ ~ ~ ~ ~ ~ ~ ~ ~ ~ ~ ~ ~

Our God Heals Again ~ ~ ~

When our children were small we were given a wonderful little toy poodle named Peppy.

*O*ur daughter, Theresa, asked me when she got married if she could take Peppy to live in her home. I said YES and thought that would be a good idea. However, one day Peppy jumped over the side of the bassinet and one of his paws apparently scratched the baby's face. Now, Theresa was very concerned for the baby's safety, so she asked me to take Peppy back; she sadly added that Peppy had lost his hearing. He was now totally deaf.

Shortly after being with us, I watched Peppy as he was walking down a hallway in our home. I snapped my fingers again and again, but there was no response. As I continued to follow Peppy, I prayed, "Lord, you *could* heal Peppy."

I snapped my fingers again, and Peppy turned around and ran to me--his hearing restored.

Isn't it wonderful that our God Loves our pets?

~ ~ ~ ~ ~ ~ ~ ~ ~ ~ ~ ~ ~ ~ ~

~ PACEMAKER HEALED ~

*O*ver 30 years ago my wife and I were traveling
with a group of tourists in Spain. Our group
stopped at a restaurant for lunch.

Lorraine and I sat at a table with a couple from Provo, Utah.
The husband began telling us that he was having serious
problems with his pacemaker, and that he was going to cut
his trip short and return home.

I asked if he wanted prayers for his failing pacemaker. Yes, he
said, and we prayed for the pacemaker, and for a safe journey
home to get medical help. But, joyfully, the pacemaker did not
malfunction after we prayed.

After arriving home, we received a letter from our friend
stating the he had the pacemaker checked out, and that it
was performing perfectly.

Thank You, Lord Jesus!

~~~~~~~~~~~~~~

*Everything comes from God alone. Everything lives by His power,
and everything is for His glory.*

*Isaiah 33:13 -- You who are far away, hear what I have done;
you who are near, acknowledge my power! (NIV)*

~~~~~~~~~~~~~~

~ CONFERENCE IN BRAZIL ~

Randy Clark *(pastor, healer and traveling
evangelist)* asked Lorraine and I
to come to Brazil for
two Christian conferences.
He repeated the invitation two more times.
We received this repeated invitation as a call from
the Lord and agreed to go.

About ten Christian Churches were involved with planning the conferences. In fact, the churches had been praying for the success of the conference for two months.

When we arrived by bus at the conference, we were greeted by a double line of people, from the bus to the soccer stadium. They escorted us to our seats located in the soccer field. There were approximately 35,000 people present, and there seemed to be a universal spirit of joy manifesting.

Conference leaders asked us to walk through the crowd and be alerted to pray for those who may need prayer. A well-dressed and sophisticated looking lady asked me to pray for her daughter who was plagued by a demon. We commanded the demon to leave her. She fell to the ground screaming and turning over and over.

After the girl recovered, she got up with a big smile on her face—she had been set free.

Then the mother told me that she, herself, had need of deliverance, saying that she had a spirit of hatred and murder. When I started to pray for her, she came at me with claw-like fingernails, intending to scratch out my eyes. I dodged her attack. But three young Brazilian women who had been trained in deliverance spotted us. They asked if I wanted help. I replied with a definite "Yes". So, they led the woman away to another location to minister deliverance, and I was relieved to have them take over the ministry, because I perceived that we were dealing with a high-leveled demon, or many demons, and deliverance that could last for hours.

~~~~~~~~~~~~~~

1 John 3:15--Anyone who hates a brother or sister is a murderer, and you know that no murderer has eternal life residing in him.

1 John: 3:23, 24--And this is His command: to believe in the name of Hs Son, Jesus Christ, and to love one another as He commanded us. The one who keeps God's commands lives in Him, and He in them. And this is how we know that He lives in us: We know it by the Spirit He gave us.(NIV)

~~~~~~~~~~~~~~

The Prayer Tent ~ ~ ~

The planners for the conference put an open-sided tent in the Northeast corner of the soccer field. The purpose of the tent was to make walk-in prayers available to all participants who had specific needs and requests.

The leader of the Prayer Ministry told me that she had two prayer teams with two members each. After we were through talking about the ministry, the leader invited me and my daughter, Theresa, to form a third team. We were given a place within the tent to pray, and three young Brazilian women to assist us by translating.

The first person who came for prayer was in a wheel-chair. We told our translator to ask the woman what she wanted us to pray for. The woman told us that she lived in a house next door to a woman that was involved with the occult. These two women got into a serious disagreement and the cultic woman put a curse on her.

She said that after she was cursed, she developed something like arthritis in most of her joints. And, said that she could no longer walk; movement of her joints was with much pain and great difficulty.

I stood close to her and prayed for the upper part of her body. I also perceived that she was under the influence of a demon. So, I commanded the demon to leave and it immediately left her. I then continued to pray for the upper part of her body, including her joints.

In the meantime, my daughter kneeled and prayed for the woman's knees and ankles. A few minutes later, during the prayers, the woman jumped out of her wheel-chair, ran forward about eight feet, did a dance, raising her arms and praising God. She apparently had been completely healed. When she left the tent, she was pushing the wheel chair.

The devil is powerful,
but our Lord is infinitely stronger and <u>all</u> powerful!

~~~~~~~~~~~~~~

Isaiah 43:10,11 – Before me no god was formed, nor will there be one after me. I, even I, am the Lord, and apart from me there is no Savior. (NIV)

~~~~~~~~~~~~~~

~ *CAN YOU BELIEVE GOD?* ~

*O*ne Sunday night, people were gathering at
Blessed Sacrament Church in Seattle
in preparation
for the Sunday Prayer Meeting.

Clara and Henry who were longtime friends, came to greet us
as we arrived. Clara told me that she had been suffering from
a painful headache. She then told me that as she came up to
greet us, she looked at my face and immediately her headache
left—*all pain was gone!*

All Glory to our Lord God, Jesus Christ!!

~ ~ ~ ~ ~ ~ ~ ~ ~ ~ ~ ~ ~

*Warning: God's Bible is habit-forming.
Regular use causes loss of anxiety,
decreased appetite for lying, cheating, stealing and hating.
Symptoms: increased sensations of love,
peace, joy and compassion.*

~ ~ ~ ~ ~ ~ ~ ~ ~ ~ ~ ~ ~

Church Musician Healed ~ ~ ~

One night at Blessed Sacrament Church, our musician stood up during the prayer meeting and exclaimed that she was a shy person and reluctant to ask for a serious prayer need until now. She said that her doctor told her she had Breast Cancer.

I then led the whole prayer group in praying for her healing. The next day she returned to her doctor who ordered an update X-Ray of her breast.

When the x-ray was completed the attendant brought the X-Ray to him. The doctor looked at the X-Ray and said, "This is the wrong X-Ray" because it did not show any signs of cancer. He told the attendant to "go back and get the right X-Ray."

The attendant went back to get the right X-Ray, but the lab had certainly received the correct one. The doctor then acknowledged that the Lord had cleansed our musician of the cancer.

~~~~~~~~~~~~~~

Romans 11:36 – For from Him and through Him and for Him are all things. To Him be the glory forever! Amen (NIV)

~~~~~~~~~~~~~~

~ LORD HEALS ARTHRITIS ~

*M*y wife was invited to speak at a church
in Silverdale, Washington.
After the talk the leader asked us to pray for
people who wanted special prayer.

A little Philippino lady came for prayer for arthritis. She told
us that she did not believe in Charismatic prayer. Then she
asked us if God would heal her even if she did not believe. I
said, "He might."

We began to pray for her arthritic condition which she said
was in the joints of her knees, ankles and hips. Again, she
asked us if God would heal her even though she did not believe
in Charismatic prayers. Again, I said that He might. A third
time she asked if God would heal her even though she did not
believe in Charismatic prayer.

I then asked her why she kept asking the same question. She
said that she thought that she was being healed. She told us
that all pain had left her body, and she confidently said that
she was really healed. Then she asked us what she should do
now that she was healed.

There were about sixteen women remaining in an adjoining
room. I told her to go into that room and announce to the
women that the Lord has just healed you. You are a witness
to our loving God's Power and Mercy—and this will be your
first testimony.

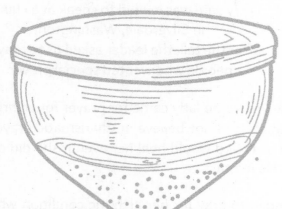

Lamentations 3:25,26 – The Lord is good to those whose hope is in Him, to the one who seeks Him; it is good to wait quietly for the salvation of the Lord. (NIV)

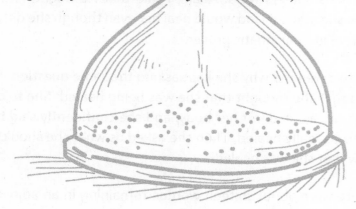

~ ANOTHER NON-BELIEVER IS HEALED ~

Several years ago--perhaps 22 or 25--our prayer group
from the Blessed Sacrament Church held
another weekend retreat.

*B*efore the first meeting began, my co-leader, 'Gene', came
to me and said that one of our members attending the retreat
was a truck-driver who had been in an accident a few days
before and was experiencing so much pain from his injuries
that he was considering returning home before the retreat
started.

He had come a long distance and had been looking forward
to the retreat experience with his Christian friends. Gene
and I approached him and asked him if he wanted to receive
prayers for healing. He said that he didn't "have enough faith
to receive that kind of healing."

I replied to him, "What do you have to lose?" And we suggested
that he could be prayed for, and if he did not get healed, then
he could go home. But, if he got healed, he would have one of
the greatest experiences of his life.

He stayed for prayer. Many of us gathered around him. After the very first prayer, he said that "all the pain left" him. He decided to stay at the retreat for the entire week-end.

The following week a member of our Prayer Group called to tell me that they met this 'unbelieving' trucker while shopping in Renton, and he reported that the Industrial Relations Board had released him to go back to work. *He had been totally healed! And, he was now a believer in our God's Power!*

~~~~~~~~~~~~~~

Isaiah 34:16 – Look in the scroll of the Lord and read. (NIV)

God's Wisdom Speaks

Proverbs 8:19 – "My fruit is better than fine gold; what I yield surpasses choice silver." (NIV)

~~~~~~~~~~~~~~

~ CLUBBED FEET HEALED ~

Long-time friends of ours lived in
Oregon City, Oregon.
Their thirteen-year-old daughter was
born with one leg
shorter than the other—
now shorter by three inches.

*T*hese dear friends heard that we had a ministry that might correct the problem. They brought their daughter to our Sunday Night Prayer Meeting at Blessed Sacrament Church, specifically for her leg to be lengthened.

The Prayer Group gathered around Kathy and prayed. Immediately the child's leg began to lengthen and become the same length as the other leg. But another healing took place that was only noticed when she tried to put on her shoes. The shoes she wore had been especially made because of the malformed condition of her feet. She had also been born with Clubbed feet, causing her to walk on the outer sides of her feet.

The grandmother called to tell us that they were going shopping at a regular shoe store because Kathy's feet were now normal, and custom-made shoes would no longer be needed.

~~~~~~~~~~~~~~

More Feet Healed ~ ~ ~

About a year later we had occasion to pray for another little 13-year-old girl who came to Seattle from Alaska especially to be prayed for. She was a cousin to Kathy. The condition of her feet was similar. Clubbed!

After the Sunday Night Prayer Group prayed for her, her feet turned to a normal position. The family was overjoyed with gratitude and was praising God.

All Glory and Praise be to our Lord God, Jesus Christ!

~ ~ ~ ~ ~ ~ ~ ~ ~ ~ ~ ~ ~

Psalm 37:23 – The Lord makes firm the steps of the one who delights in him; although he may stumble, he will not fall, for the Lord upholds him with his hand.

~ ~ ~ ~ ~ ~ ~ ~ ~ ~ ~ ~ ~

~ SPIRITUAL AWAKENING ~

One year Lorraine and I traveled
to Medgegoria, Croatia.
This was a time of great spiritual awakening.

*W*e stayed at the home of a visionary's brother. Two unusual events, among many, took place during our stay.

1- I had thrown my back out of alignment and was suffering considerable pain, not able to walk to the event's site, and it was difficult for me to get in and out of a taxi.

Maria, one of the visionaries, came to her brother's house where we were staying. She gave a talk to the people staying in the house and prayed for each person. When she got to me, she prayed for my back and it was instantly healed.

2- A young boy's face and head began to swell, and it was painful. He knew he was allergic to peanuts and any food containing them and that he must avoid them.

The candy bar that he was eating didn't appear to have peanuts in it. However, on carefully reading the label, the candy bar's contents were processed with **peanut oil**—being just as dangerous to this young child's life—perhaps even more so.

Maria and other members of the Prayer Team were called to prayer, and they surrounded him, and as we watched, the swelling began to diminish, and it finally disappeared completely. The child could breathe normally and see with normal vision once again.

Thank you, Lord God!

1 Corinthians 2:9 – What no eye has seen, what no ear has heard, and what no human mind has conceived, the things God has prepared for those who love Him. (NIV)

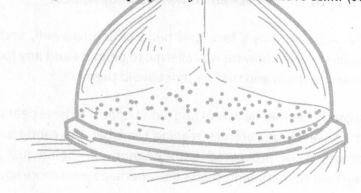

~ INVASION OF THE WARTS ~

In the mid-1980's I had many warts attacking my body.
They were growing under my fingernails,
bottoms of my feet, backs of
my hands and on toes.

I tried different kinds of wart removal medicine, but it had no effect. Then Lorraine and I attended a couple's retreat at the Warm Beach Camp at Stanwood, Washington.

During one of the services, Dick Mills *(now deceased)* the retreat leader, invited those people who needed healing to come forward. He announced that although he was not a healer, the Lord told him that all those who had come for healing would be healed. When my wife heard this, she gave me a couple of elbows to my ribs to get me up for prayer.

I was prayed for, but nothing seemed to happen. And when I returned to my seat beside my wife, she told me that she thought that I had been healed. My response to her was "that sure was a rare type of healing" because I still had all the warts.

The following day she again told me that she believed that I was healed.

On the third day she once again told me that I was healed but that I was too stubborn to receive it. Lorraine was so adamant on the healing of my warts that I began to believe she had information that I didn't.

I decided to take some time to pray about this matter. I told the Lord that if He had a healing for my wart condition that I was not receiving because of my unbelief, I repent of that unbelief and was willing to receive whatever He had for me.

The very next day I noticed that two warts on the back of my hand had changed color. The substance of the warts had changed to a fine powder. When I wiped off the powder I saw new, healthy skin. Both warts had completely disappeared.

When I counted the warts, I found that I had 32, plus another 12 that surrounded the middle toe of my right foot. For the next several days the warts started 'healing' —one or two at a time. Finally, all the warts were gone except for the colony of warts on my middle toe.

I did not realize that my wife was in the room when I took off the sock from my right foot, the one with the toe covered with warts. She spotted my weird looking toe and said, "What is that?" Then, as I began to explain that my middle toe has a covering of warts, the warts all exploded at the same time and fell to the floor.

My middle toe now was cleansed of every wart and showed new fresh skin. From that time on I never had another wart.

When I began to witness about my healing from the warts, people began to ask to have their wart conditions prayed for. Without any advertising, people were coming to Blessed Sacrament Prayer Meetings for healing of their wart conditions—people from north Seattle, Camano Island, Whidbey Island and even from areas within the San Juan Islands. All were healed...

And, it is here that we once again say - -
Thank you to our most Merciful and
Powerful Lord God, Jesus!

~~~~~~~~~~~~~~

~ *NEW MEXICO MIRACLE* ~

*S*everal years ago we were corresponding with friends, a married couple who had been living in Renton, Washington, when we first met. But now they were retired and had moved to New Mexico. Several times this couple invited us to visit them.

Finally, we accepted their kind invitation; and we drove to their beautiful home in a new housing development in Rio Rancho.

Our hostess, drew up a list of people she wanted us to pray for. The first person on the list had cancer throughout his body. He had been an usher and helper at a nearby Catholic church—faithfully assisting at the church for over twenty years. And, she told us more about this man's condition, that shortly before our arrival this man had "something mysterious" happen to him.

FIRST, his whole body became filled with cancer so quickly. THEN, he lost his faith in the goodness of God—believing that he was going to spend his whole life in an eternal hell. AND, he told us that he no longer believed in Christian prayers, so he did not want prayers said for him.

We were unable to get him to reject these false beliefs that were plaguing his thinking. It was unbelievable to Lorraine and me to hear this man talk so casually and matter-of-factly about 'going to hell' as being acceptable—even to be joyous about it.

After we returned home, we received news that the man had lapsed into a coma and was taken to the local hospital. The organs of his body were swollen and retaining massive amounts of fluid.

Family members were called and invited to be present during his final hours; and so they gathered around his bed. Although he had told everyone that he did not want prayers, a priest was called to perform the rites anyway. As the priest prayed, great amounts of fluids began flowing from the man's body, soaking the sheets that covered the bed and his body and the floor surrounding the hospital bed.

And, as the family watched, this man came out of the comatose state, and he clearly said, "I want to go to church." And they witnessed that as he said this, 'his body was returning to its normal size'. Later, those who watched this transformation also said that he was completely healed of cancer and "indeed, he returned to church."

It's never too late to turn to God!
It's never too late for God, our merciful and glorious Savior Jesus Christ, to make Himself known to us, and heal us of whatever sickness or disease we are suffering.

~ ~ ~ ~ ~ ~ ~ ~ ~ ~ ~ ~ ~ ~

~ ~ *Be Blessed, In His Time* ~ ~

All of the writers and believers have
experienced and enjoyed the presence of
God and His wondrous ways. You can too.

Psalm 85:8-9 -- I will listen to what God the Lord says;
He promises peace to His people, His faithful
servants—but let them not turn to folly. Surely
His salvation is near those who fear Him, that
His Glory may dwell in our land. (NIV)

AMEN